It's only the Vicar

Harold Hosking

First published by Gooday Publishers, Chichester, West Sussex 1987

© Harold Hosking 1987

All rights reserved. No part of this publication may be reproduced or transmitted in any form or by any means, electronic or mechanical, including photocopying, recording, or any information storage and retrieval system, without permission in writing from the publisher.

British Library Cataloguing in Publication Data

Hoskin, Harold
 It's only the vicar : tales from a Cornish fishing community a quarter of a century ago.
 1. Fishers - England - Penzance (Cornwall)
 2. Newlyn (Penzance, Cornwall) - Social life and customs
 3. Penzance (Cornwall) - Social life and customs
 I. Title
 942.3'75   DA690.P4

ISBN 1-87056-801-X

Printed by Caligraving Limited
Thetford, Norfolk, England

Contents

New Bishop	1
New Parish	20
Newlyn	31
Day by Day	41
Getting Organised	57
A Feel of the Sea	66
Morwenna	79
Letter from America	86
Home again	94
'To Everything There is a Time'	102
Epilogue	109

Foreword

It is inevitable that an autobiography should show only one man's point of view, in this case that of a parish priest. I am glad to have been asked to write a foreword, because I had the luck to work in Newlyn at the time Canon Hosking was Vicar there. I was invariably struck by the fact that, when any sort of crisis occurred, the cry was always "Where's Vicar?" A sobering experience for the family doctor. Hence the fund of splendid stories - only possible from an incomparably good Parish Priest. The flavour of Old Cornwall as it was before so many of us 'foreigners' crossed the Tamar to live in this lovely county.

Rosemary Rostron
Pentrig, Lelant, St. Ives.
1987

New Bishop

Spring comes to Cornwall exceptionally early in some years. Though gales can lash our Cornish coast at almost any time of year, and the rain comes teeming in from the Atlantic, it can all change in a moment to one of those balmy days with quite warm sunshine as early as the latter part of February. It was a day like that in 1956 when I set out accompanied by Doreen my wife, for Carnanton House in the parish of St. Mawgan, where we were to be the guests of Colonel and Mrs. Willyams.

This was not just a social occasion, although it was most enjoyable to be entertained to lunch by such charming people in their stately home. I had been invited to look at the parish of St. Mawgan by Colonel Willyams, the patron of the living, at the suggestion of our saintly Bishop Edmund Morgan, with the possibility in mind that I might become the next incumbent. Little did I realise that day all that this might involve me in.

Carnanton stands on a kind of plateau and, because of this, it was an ideal place for an aerodrome, a fact quickly recognized by the Royal Air Force. The runways of R.A.F. St. Mawgan come right up to the sweeping lawns which surround the old manor house. The thickly wooded valley extends away in the general direction of Mawgan Porth passing through the lovely vale of Lanherne. This is an unusual sight in North Cornwall just a mile or two from the sea.

In the early afternoon we all set out for the village of

It's Only the Vicar

St. Mawgan with the local people eyeing us with considerable curiosity. At that time it was still very much a village which had seen little in the way of change or development, and one could say it was still unspoilt.

One of the first buildings that caught my eye was the Carmelite convent standing on one side of the valley, above the church, partly hidden by beautiful beech trees. The old manor house had been given to the nuns as a place of refuge, at the end of the French Revolution, by the Arundel family as they fled from Antwerp. These dear ladies must have appeared in excellent condition, with no signs of fasting, since they brought with them some priceless vestments - concealed beneath their habits! These vestments are still to be seen on special occasions and the kindly sisters of this enclosed order are always most gracious and helpful, in spite of the fact that they themselves are never seen.

Our hosts took us to the Falcon Inn to meet the lady of the house, a certain Mrs. Fry then in her eighties and every bit the grand old Victorian character you would expect to see in a picture gallery. The inn stands in an old country garden with a magnificent magnolia tree. Between the convent and the inn stands the old parish church which was of course, of great interest to me at that particular moment. We approached through the lychgate on the east and I noted the graceful proportions of the tower which stands at the south side of the church, a most unusual feature in Cornwall. Entering the church my first impression was the sense of peace, an atmosphere which seemed to say that generation after generation had worshipped here, hallowing it for all who enter.

I should be fortunate indeed if I were offered the opportunity to serve here as the parish priest. There were, of course, things of special interest including a pre-Reformation Screen, an ancient font, a Mary Tudor pulpit, many fine bench ends, some striking stained glass and some very fine brasses.

But so it transpired in the summer of 1956 it was my great joy and privilege to be instituted to the living in that

New Bishop

old parish church by the Bishop. The living had become vacant through the sudden death of my predecessor the Revd. John Arthur Chesterton (a relative of the famous G.K. Chesterton). He had been found dead in his study in the rectory. Doreen, our daughter Ruth and myself moved in to make this place our home. To say that it was empty when we arrived would not be quite correct since an owl, many bats and at least one rat were already in residence.

It was a stately house with fine reception rooms, eight bedrooms, servants' quarters, a butler's pantry and very spacious cellar. The outbuildings included a stable, with well-equipped loose boxes, and an adjoining coach house. It was all very lovely and enjoyable during the summer months but a cold and lonely place throughout the winter. Sounds from the village below helped! The regular chiming of the church clock was comforting and perhaps, more especially, the sound of the children in the school playground.

In the village school, the good headmaster, his wife and an assistant teacher devoted themselves to the work of educating the local children. Their interest went far beyond the school building and the regular hours of teaching, for they were concerned for each child and for the family to which they belonged. They were also fully integrated into the life of the community. At Christmas time they would be an essential part of the nativity play in the parish church and they would also take the older children carol-singing around the parish. The highlight of this perambulation would be at Carnanton House where, after the carol singing, all would be invited to come in and to partake of liberal refreshments. One could never forget the look on the faces of some of the children as they entered this stately home for the first time and looked up with awe at the winding staircase and the painted ceilings. Life in St. Mawgan was varied and enjoyable. Born a countryman, I could appreciate the country life, talk the language and take my place beside men at work in the harvest field. At such times men loved to talk of past days and, in particular, past rectors. Although my immediate predecessor had been with them for more

It's Only the Vicar

than a decade, we heard little about him save some amusing anecdotes and many tributes to his skill as an artist and his brilliant oratory.

In contrast, the older generation constantly spoke of "Dear Old Canon". This was a reference to Canon Gunning who was greatly loved and had evidently left his mark on the parish. Occasionally there were those who would go back as far as "Father Wayne" and to whom they referred as a "real gentleman who had a curate to do the work!"

St. Mawgan was my first parish and I remember with gratitude those who guided and helped me so much at that time. We were blessed with two keen and conscientious churchwardens as well as Colonel Neynoe Willyams who was not only the patron but also a devout churchman who gave his backing to whatever I attempted for the good of the parish.

Then there were three sisters, Misses Hawkey. They ran the shop next to the Falcon Inn and the whole community owed them a debt. They were there it seemed, not only to serve in their little shop, but to be of service to everyone in need. If there were a parcel to be left, a child to be looked after, a message to be passed or some information sought, everyone turned to the Misses Hawkey at The Shop. I am forever grateful to them for the help they gave to our little family and for the amount of information they imparted to me. They were a mine of information about the local community, and that information was always given in confidence and with the utmost charity.

Not long after I was inducted the senior of these three sisters told me about a man who was very ill and should be visited. Following carefully her instructions I found my way to a little house where there was only the faintest light shining through the darkness. Even before I got to the door I could hear what the local people would refer to as "the death rattles". Alone in a downstairs room I found a man. I saw at a glance that he had once been of very fine physique. Now nearing the end of his life, to all intents unconscious, he was fighting for breath and in a bath of perspiration. As I held his hands and prayed with him I heard a tapping at the window pane and, on going closer, I could make out the face of a man. I signalled him around to the back door and he came in and stood with me, evidently feeling at a loss for anything to say or do. "Are you a relative?" I asked.

"Son," he replied tersely, and then, after a long pause, "We've had our differences in the family since he took to drink and we haven't seen a lot of each other."

"Well, I'm glad you are here now," I said, "Let's make something of this reconciliation." Soon after the poor man died.

In the three or four years that followed I saw quite a lot of his widow as well as other members of this family well-known throughout the district. His brother and his nephew were highly-skilled craftsmen, as were nearly all the males who carried this particular name, their speciality being the art of Cornish stone-hedging. To say that they were outspoken would be putting it mildly but I enjoyed their company and found them ready to give their services wherever it would benefit the church.

During the next four-and-a-half years I shared the life of that community, their joys as well as their sorrows. Quite often tragic circumstances were interwoven with quite a lot of humour. One Friday evening, the eve of a wedding, I was on my way through the village to say Evensong and heard a rumour that the wedding had been called off.

"Have you heard anything Rector?"

"Not a thing," I replied.

"Well! He's bought a tin of rat poison and is going to do himself in if she jilts him now," I was warned. Evensong was a little shorter after that communication.

Arriving at the back door of the rectory I met the unfortunate couple. I was a little taken back to see that they were in the company of our local police constable. He asked to have a private word with me, and went on to explain the situation. He had been summoned to the girl's home when, after he had been told the wedding was off, the pending bridegroom had become difficult.

"He tells me," the policeman explained, "that he has taken a bottle of aspirins and if he gets the opportunity, he's going to finish it off properly. It makes me feel a bit responsible," he added. His purpose in bringing them to the rectory was that I might have a word with them so that something might be sorted out.

Knowing something of the would-have-been-bride and her sense of the dramatic I suggested that I should first of all have a word with her on her own.

"Well, my dear, are you, or are you not getting married tomorrow?" I put the question to her without any frills.

"I'll not marry him tomorrow, nor ever," came the emphatic reply.

"Then you need not waste any more of our time and you can go home at once," I suggested. Very soon the plump little figure was to be seen trotting up the rectory drive. As it transpired, that however, was the least of our worries. The good constable and myself were left with a distraught and unfortunate man on our hands. We took him to the study in an attempt to bring some calm and reason to him in his unhappy situation. This was to prove more difficult than we had first assumed.

However we had a doctor newly-arrived in the parish who was keen and energetic. I telephoned him and outlined the situation with the request that I might just bring our patient along.

"Keep him with you," was the answer, "I'll be right there." He had arrived in a matter of minutes, confirmed that it was evident that he had taken an overdose and asked my wife for a glass of salt and warm water.

"Drink this," the doctor ordered, "And I'm afraid in a few minutes you will be very sick."

I saw why the doctor had thought it best to deal with the matter in my study rather than his own home! We waited, but nothing happened, except our erstwhile bridegroom swung his studded belt around more and more alarmingly.

New Bishop

The constable decided that he had had enough of this and decided that it was time to ring the sergeant at St. Columb Major. It was about an hour before this senior officer of the law arrived. He was a huge man and took the situation over with complete authority.

"Have you searched him to see that there is nothing more on him that he can take?" was the first question.

"No," we replied and the process was soon accomplished amid many protestations from one who, but for the whims of a silly girl, might have been one of the happiest men in the county at that time.

"Now doctor," the sergeant continued, "Is it possible to give him something that will quieten him down and make him sleep for the night?"

"I can give him something that will put him out like a light, if that is what you wish," came the reply.

"You said, doctor, that I would be sick more than an hour ago, and that hasn't happened yet," came the quick rejoinder.

At that very moment, and it may have been the very mention of the word 'sick' that had something to do with it, I saw him turn very pale. I immediately suggested that this was the time for us to walk alone in the drive to consider the "theological implications" of what he was intending! The timing could not have been better and we had not gone far before I was giving thanks that the involuntary emptying of his stomach was now taking place in the open air rather than in the confines of the rectory!

Rejoining the little party in the study we found the sergeant had had a little time for reflection.

"Where do you come from, boy?" he asked as we entered.

"Bugle," came the sullen reply.

"Has your father got a milk round?"

There was a nod of the head to indicate his agreement.

Drawing on his wide experience, the sergeant had decided it was time the family were involved. He had a theory that it was wrong to have the police force, the doctor and the parson on the run while our man's own family were comfortably at home asleep. A phone call to the particular home in Bugle soon brought a van to the rectory. Before loading the rejected bridegroom into it, the constable was ordered to accompany him to the girl's home to pick up any of his belongings. He returned with several "bits and pieces", including some pillow-cases in their cellulose wrappings, ribbons and all, as well as two oven-ready chicken in a string bag - a present from his boss for the wedding breakfast. With a wry smile, the sergeant suggested that one chicken might go to the doctor and the other to the rector as some kind of compensation. We did not press the point, being only too sorry for the one who was victim of these circumstances, and all too happy to see the milk van receding up the drive at a somewhat unusual hour for such a vehicle.

I have often had occasion to thank the wisdom of that particular police sergeant since that time. All too often we chase around looking for various 'departments' to deal with some situation which really belongs within the family and can best be dealt with there with the minimum of outside support.

Parts of our parish were, inevitably, affected by the tourist trade, notably Mawgan Porth and Watergate Bay. While life in the village remained quite constant we saw the effects of the summer and winter seasons in these resorts. One of the results was we were able to use a cafe for our Sunday School during the winter months through the generosity of the owners. One Sunday afternoon we had just assembled and I noted that there were one or two fresh faces. This was nothing unusual since R.A.F. families were constantly on the move. We joined together for the opening prayers, hymns and a brief talk and then I went across to the eldest of the newly-arrived to conduct him to the Bible Class. It was then that I noticed he held a ten-shilling note in his hand.

"Look," he said, with some disgust, "I didn't come in for this you know, I only wanted a bottle of pop."

In the village itself we had coach parties that made for the Parish Church as one of the places of interest. I was

New Bishop

just coming out of the vestry when I heard one coach party arrive. They were being conducted on their tour by the driver and I was full of curiosity to hear just what he told them on their guided tour.

"Here," he began, "Right inside the door is a list of the rectors of this place from the twelfth century down to the present time." At that precise moment he caught sight of me hiding in the doorway and, without a pause, he went on, "Here before you is the present holder of that office and he will now be pleased to tell you all about this ancient church." I humbly played my part as though all this had been carefully arranged on their behalf.

A confirmation is always a great day in the life of any parish, and certainly at St. Mawgan it was no exception. The months of preparation by the candidates led to the great occasion when the Bishop came for the Laying on of Hands. Over the years a tradition had grown up at St. Mawgan as to the pattern to be followed on the great day. The service in church took place at 7 p.m. and then the congregation would retire to the Church Hall (actually an ancient tithe barn). There the candidates and their families would meet the Bishop over a cup of tea and refreshments. What, however, made the occasion unique was that following the gathering in the hall, the Bishop and his wife, together with the rector and his wife, were entertained to dinner at Carnanton by Colonel and Mrs. Willyams.

One year, after the candidates had been under instruction for a few weeks, we learned that Bishop Edmund Morgan was to retire, and that we would have to wait for his successor. Bishop Maurice Key, the Suffragan Bishop of Sherbourne, was to come to Truro as our new Diocesan and he offered to come to us for the confirmation and follow the usual pattern of procedure. We were pleased to be among the first to have a visit from our new Bishop, and everything was put in hand to assure him of a warm welcome.

We were all greatly impressed when the imposing figure came into the ancient church in cope and mitre, and he seemed to fill the whole place with his presence. His strong voice and easy manner soon made us all, including the candidates, feel perfectly at ease and we were able to listen with real interest to an address which went quickly to the essentials. The service over, the people of the parish delighted in meeting Bishop and Mrs. Key in the happy and relaxed atmosphere which marks such occasions. Now the time had come for us to go to Carnanton and the Bishop and his wife went on ahead with their hosts. Doreen and I followed soon after.

I well remember being greeted by the Colonel in his usual open manner.

"The ladies have gone upstairs," he said, "If you are wanting to go to the toilet you'll have to wait because the Bishop is using mine." This was a very specially-equipped toilet at the rear of the Colonel's study.

The ladies then came downstairs and joined us for drinks. Time passed and we made cheerful conversation but there was no sign of the Bishop. Time went on - ten minutes, a quarter of an hour. Nobody said anything but there must have been various thoughts about what episcopal complications were delaying his lordship.

Just as some concern was about to be expressed, a commotion was heard coming from the servants quarters. These were occupied at that time by a Polish family which acted as butler, cook, housekeeper and all those other domestic roles in a household of that nature. It was at that moment that our genial host exploded, "Dammit, I believe I locked the Bishop in the toilet!"

This was indeed the case. Without thinking and quite automatically he had put the bolt across as he went through the study. The poor Bishop, realizing his predicament had climbed out of the window (no mean feat for a man of his stature). He had then made his way through the shrubs to the only light that he could see. Looking in at the window he had truly startled the little Polish family.

However all was well and the party complete, we went in to enjoy our meal. At various intervals during dinner one could see the Colonel's shoulders start to heave and his suppressed laughter would then break forth as he again apologised to his guest, who only too readily joined in the fun. During that evening we discovered what a very human, loving and humble pastor had taken over as Diocesan Bishop of Truro.

From what happened soon after this, I pondered whether the Bishop had found time to put his mind to other things than being locked up in solitary confinement, for he was to take a hand in my life.

Meanwhile, blissfully unaware of any thoughts which were germinating in the Bishop's mind, we soldiered on in the parish. New ventures were in hand to meet particular needs. A coach was hired to bring residents, especially the younger generation, to the church from Mawgan Porth for the family service each Sunday morning. At Trevarrian, one of the hamlets near Watergate Bay, we held regular services on a Sunday evening in the large room of one of the farm houses. All the time we were getting to know people and were able to share fully in the life of the community.

Our nearest neighbour was Lady Geraldine Boyle, of whom some of the school children had written, "What we like about Lady Geraldine is that she isn't a bit like a lady." Those who knew this charming lady knew that it was most kindly meant.

She was a very keen member of our branch of the Guild of St. Raphael, which is one of the church's branches for the ministry of healing. Lady G was of the opinion that we should not only meet for prayer and discussion but that we ought to be quite practical and lend help wherever it was needed.

An opportunity was not far to seek. At that time we had in the parish a family of eleven children, and their home was badly in need of some interior decoration. One afternoon her Ladyship and I set out with the necessary paint.

"Don't worry about the dogs," I reassured her, "The one that bites is safely chained up and the other just makes a lot of noise." Going through the yard I was dismayed to see, what I had never seen before - the wrong dog was running loose. I said nothing, but just went on, hoping. Certainly I need not have worried on Lady Geraldine's account for she just went striding on. But as I followed I felt teeth come through my coat and clamp firmly into my arm. "Everything all right?" she asked.

Another colourful character was our honorary treasurer, Major Ralph Liddicoat. He, too, was a member of the Guild of St. Raphael and made sure that, while our heads might sometimes have been in the clouds, our feet stayed firmly on the ground. He was very informal and at times a little unorthodox. On Easter Day, after Evensong he would come into the rectory and plant a bag of money on the table and say, "There, that's yours." So much nicer than a cheque handed in a week or two later!

He had his heart in the right place too. At the annual church meeting of our fourth year it was discovered that we had had a very good year and could show a very substantial balance. Ralph immediately proposed that we give half of it to the missionary societies. It was good to have people like Ralph Liddicoat on our Church Council. Indeed our meetings were nearly always happy occasions where we enjoyed the fellowship and got through the business without rancour or fuss.

One item which came on to the agenda did cause a certain amount of disquiet. It was the question of what to do about a huge sycamore tree standing in the churchyard and quite near to the east end of the church itself. It had stood there for generations - nobody knew quite how long. The problem now was that it had grown too large and the sheer weight of the overhanging branches was lifting part of the churchyard as it tilted towards the road beneath. Reluctantly it was decided that it must come down, but our difficulty was finding someone who would tackle the job of felling it. It was, to say the least, a tricky business being so close to the church, the road and the Falcon Inn.

After numerous enquiries we found a man from Little Petherick who, on condition we found someone to do the winching, was ready to undertake the work. Headstones were moved in preparation, and then the great day arrived.

New Bishop

I was told that the sycamore should be down by 10 o'clock that morning but, because of the snags, it still stood there, defiantly, at 2 p.m. By this time the school children had all assembled up the road at a safe distance to watch the fall of this giant of a landmark.

At 2.30 p.m., just as Colonel Willyams had arrived from a sitting of the bench at St. Columb, there was a resounding bang. The tree seemed to turn as it split up the middle and then shuddered for a moment before falling across the lychgate at the same time demolishing the mausoleum of the Willyams family. Roof and granite wall came down with the tree, and fifteen lead coffins lay open to the sky. It was a dramatic moment and one I shall never forget. It was a great relief to me, and indeed to us all, when the good Colonel looked over the wall at the devastation and said, "I'll bet that made old grandad jump!"

I spent a rather restless night contemplating where the money would come from to put matters right. The unfortunate tree-feller was not insured and it was hardly right that anyone but the Church Council should pay, but we had not really got that kind of money. Inspiration came in the early hours of the morning. I remembered our insurance with the Ecclesiastical Insurance Office. Very soon a letter was on its way. They readily accepted responsibility for a third party claim and I was able to spend some time talking the matter over with Colonel Willyams.

As usual he was full of good common sense and suggested that we should not rebuild something which would be very costly and a burden on future generations. We decided to bury the coffins at the same spot and erect a simple granite cross over them. This now stands there, a simple and dignified memorial to this notable family.

It seemed at that time that life was very full. Our daughter was very happy at the little school and delighted to come up the lane in the evenings to greet her pony. The changing seasons were a great joy in these lovely parts and we had happy relationships with both the Roman Catholics and the Methodists. It seemed that I should be staying even longer than 'Dear Old Canon'.However this was not to be.

New Parish

There is always something special about what you are told as a great secret, particularly when there is quite a bit more involved that you do not know. A former Archdeacon of Bodmin and friend of our family for many years telephoned me with a piece of news in the utmost confidence to the effect that the Dean and Chapter would like to offer me a certain living. This, in itself was most interesting but there was something more.

The Bishop had asked them to "hold their hand" until he had seen me and discussed something else. What this other "something" might be I was most curious to hear about, although, at this stage, I was not terribly interested in moving elsewhere.

I had not long to wait before I received a letter from the Bishop of Truro with a request that I should come and see him. So it was that I found myself in his study waiting to hear what he had to say. He wanted me to consider moving to Newlyn in West Cornwall where, as he put it, I would find plenty of scope for my energy and enthusiasm. He then went on to outline what would be involved in this most interesting parish. It was then left to me to go away and think about it, to go and see Newlyn and, above all to say my prayers about the matter before coming to see him again.

My wife and I went to Newlyn to look at the parish, including the two churches and the vicarage. As we passed over the little bridge in Newlyn Coombe to see St. Peter's

New Parish

Church we were struck by what we saw in the stream - any amount of debris including old fish boxes and quite a number of fish-heads. It was all too easy to contrast this with the picturesque stream we had left behind at our home in St. Mawgan.

A glance at the church showed that a lot of essential work needed to be done. In fact, plans were already in hand to launch an appeal fund to save the fabric and instal a new heating system. Inside, the beauty of the little church was overshadowed by the need for a good spring-clean and redecoration. When we saw the vicarage our hearts went out to the previous incumbent who must have endured an uncomforable four years and more there, living as a bachelor. It was in a terrible state of repair with dampness showing everywhere. It proved so bad that much of it had to be pulled down.

Sister Alice of the Community of the Epiphany, who was then working in the parish, was waiting to receive us in the church hall. Happy and jovial, she certainly brought some warmth into our visit but, when she took us downstairs we were again struck by the awful feeling of dampness and cold. She took us to the Mission Church of St. Andrew, near Penlee Quarry. This proved to be a delightful little building with a lot of warmth and atmosphere although, here again, much needed to be done in the way of essential repairs. One problem was that every time they blasted at the quarry a little more plaster fell from the roof.

Back at St. Mawgan we began to feel how fortunate we were to live in such lovely surroundings, and already ideas were turning over in my mind as to what I should say to the Bishop when next we met.

When that meeting came, however, things did not turn out just as I had imagined them in my own mind. I began with a well-prepared statement.

"Yes, my Lord, Newlyn looks very exciting, and indeed challenging, in so many ways, but there are so many things that I have just begun at St. Mawgan that I feel sure I ought to see these established before I leave."

"Of course," replied the Bishop with a very knowing smile. "And if you stay for five, or even ten years I expect it would be just the same."

I had the feeling that his Lordship felt it right and proper that I should go to Newlyn, and without more ado, I said that perhaps this was the case. He confirmed that this was indeed exactly what he did feel, and there and then I accepted his offer of the living.

Some of us in the Church of England feel that we should in such circumstances accept without question whatever our Bishop deems to be right. If we profess to the authority of the Church, then we ourselves should be happy to live within that discipline. Legally, I could have turned down the offer but I could not in all good conscience go against the wishes of the Bishop. This would seem to point to the fact that the Bishop of the diocese is, in most cases, the person best suited to appoint clergy to their various benefices.

There are, of course, other patrons who have, for generations, carried out their responsibilities with care and true insight. Yet, provided the Bishop has had the time to know his diocese and his clergy, is a man of wisdom as well as of prayer and is, in addition, willing to consult with the senior clergy in the diocese about matters of which they have special knowledge, then the appointments can surely be left with him. In the years which followed I had every reason to be thankful that I had put my trust and confidence in Bishop Maurice Key.

We were delighted to find that plans were soon to be put in hand to make the vicarage at Newlyn more comfortable, and Canon Arthur Williams, then Rural Dean, was on the spot to make some valuable suggestions and see that they were carried out. I did not relish the thought of going to tell the Patron at St. Mawgan what was planned, but I need not have feared. He and his wife were both most kind and, with the rest of the parish gave us a wonderful send-off. Among the few things we treasure in our home is a silver tray, suitably inscribed, which was presented to us by Colonel and Mrs. Willyams as their personal memento.

New Parish

Owing to the amount of work needing to be done at Newlyn vicarage, our move was not immediate. We arrived there just before Easter 1961. The induction service proved to be a new experience for me in many ways. At St. Mawgan it had been very much for the faithful of the parish but here in Newlyn we were part of the Borough of Penzance. This meant the service was attended by various dignitaries, as well as representative clergy from the large Deanery of Penwith and beyond. The Mayor of Penzance was accompanied by the Town Clerk, and the Member of Parliament for St. Ives was also present; so, too, was the Chief Inspector of Police. We were certainly not able to forget the fact that Newlyn was a harbour and fishing community. The Superintendent of the Royal National Mission to Deep Sea Fishermen was there, together with Harbour Commissioners, fishermen, and the Commander of the Trinity House Vessel, the Satellite.

At this time I became aware of the value of Sister Alice as well as of our two churchwardens. One of the churchwardens, Joe Stevens, not only held this important office but he possessed a fine bass voice and was therefore a valued member of the choir. If need be, he could also put on a red cassock and take his place among the servers in the sanctuary. The other warden, Arthur Richards, was one of those remarkable characters who seem to be almost indispensable - never ruffled and always cheerful and willing under all circumstances. It seemed one had only to think hard enough about something which needed to be done, especially if there was a hammer and some hard work involved, and it was well under way.

This was typical. Coming home for tea one evening I chatted to Arthur outside the church for a minute or two. I made a remark about the dilapidated condition of the fence, comprising some iron railings and box shrubs. During tea, my wife looked out of the window and exclaimed, "Whatever is going on out in the drive?"

"Nothing, as far as I know," I confessed.

"Well, you had better take a look, because it appears as though there has been a bulldozer at work there for the last

It's Only the Vicar

hour or two," I was told. Going to satisfy my curiosity I found that Arthur had set about the fence with a will; iron work lay in a tangled mass in the drive while all the shrubs had been uprooted. "But I had only expressed it as a passing thought that we might one day raise this at a church council meeting," I began.

"No use waiting for that," said our enthusiastic churchwarden without pausing from what he was doing. "You've got to get on with it while it's fresh in your mind."

The evenings during the rest of that week were spent in taking down two large pillars which stood at the entrance to the bridge and making them up into little pillars to stand on concrete bases. To complete the job we put some lengths of chain between each pillar. Much of the work we did in the dark with the help of a local boat-builder and it was little wonder that our neighbour across the road pointed out that some pillars were quite close to one another while others were far apart.

"To give it a rustic effect in front of the church," we explained, glibly.

As I reflect upon this kind of activity in which we often engaged, both inside and outside the church, I do so with a certain amount of satisfaction, and certainly I have no pangs of conscience about not always following the rules.

While I will admit that a certain amount of control over church architecture is desirable, having to obtain Archdeacon's Certificates and Faculties before any move can be made, I do believe has often been taken to ridiculous extremes. Often we have listened to charges and had to read reams of literature which seemed to place more emphasis on bricks and mortar, gravestones and brass tablets, than the proclamation of the Kingdom of Heaven. The present generation is growing impatient with some old patterns of worship, and with concern over the non-essentials in buildings, and is looking for a fresh and vigorous way forward. Very soon after my induction I became aware that we had not only come among a very close-knit community, but also that we could only be accepted within that community by being loving and caring.

New Parish

The Saturday after my arrival I had a wedding in the early afternoon. While there is nothing unusual about that, it meant that I was faced with one of those finely-balanced decisions which have to be taken all too quickly. All the guests were in church, the groom and the best man were in their proper places, the organ played while some nervous bridesmaids waited in the porch.

Just at that moment a lady came rushing up to me, very much out-of-breath. Could I come at once and administer Holy Communion to a relative who was very ill? After asking one or two questions about his condition, I decided the wedding should come first and that I would come to the house at the earliest possible moment after the registers had been signed.

That turned out to be the right decision for I was still taking the good man his Communion for many years to follow. It was just as well for me, for, had I decided the other way, I should have certainly got off on the wrong foot with a considerable section of the local community.

The following day was, of course, my first Sunday in the Parish and it is always interesting to see how full the church can be on such occasions when people come along to see just what kind of 'animal' they have acquired.

The end of the day did bring some light relief. As I stood in the porch shaking the hands of the people as they departed a little lady stepped briskly forward. "May I introduce myself," she began, "The name is Hawkins and I am a descendant of the famous Admiral." 'Descent', was certainly the operative word, for, as she spoke the elastic in her skirt gave way and that part of her attire dropped instantly to the floor. Her distinguished ancestor would have been proud of her at that moment as she acted in the greatest tradition of the Senior Service by stepping neatly over the fallen article and with great decorum placed it over her arm and retreated gracefully to the vicarage to make the necessary adjustment.

Already I was beginning to meet some of the colourful characters who made up this unique community. They were people who took great pride in the fact that they belonged to Newlyn, and even to particular parts of this little town. You may belong to Newlyn Town or 'Street-a-Nowen'. To belong to Mousehole wasn't too bad, but to confess that you came from St. Ives took some courage and you may well be referred to as an "Ake". There was a great advantage in all this for, although Newlyn had now grown considerably in size, the parish taking in both Alverton and the estates around the Bowjey, people still lived in what might be termed 'village communities'. This had the effect of giving a true sense of neighbourliness with people truly caring about those who still lived in the same row or terrace. Again and again in later years I would go to call on someone I knew to be elderly or infirm and would hardly have knocked on the door before a head would pop out of a window or around a door to inform me where I could find 'Uncle Ben' or 'Aunt Hilda'.

This proved to be a caring and sharing community where people who lived close together were very often close friends, if not actually related. You learned quickly to tread warily and to be careful about passing remarks about individuals.

While it was unwise for me to make any comments or pass opinions on local people, there were those who knew how to be quite outspoken. One old lady who had once been very active in the life of the church was now housebound and lived with her cousin. On one of my visits we were in her little sitting-room, talking, while her cousin could be heard moving around in the next room. The old dear started by telling me how good her cousin was in looking after her, and then came what one of my predecessors used to refer to as "The Newlyn BUT". At the top of her voice she concluded this tribute to her illustrious relative by saying, "But she's a rogue, a thief and a liar." I was hardly sitting comfortably for the rest of my visit.

The more one saw of these people the greater the confidence grew between us, and they were most appreciative of any little pastoral ministrations that one could offer. They were people who had known hard times

New Parish

and lived through them. There were men and women who could recall sanded floors and fish salted in the box in the corner to last them through the winter. Indeed there were still marks in the houses where dampness appeared because of the salt left in the plaster marks which refused to be covered up by decoration.

Singing was very much part of the life of Newlyn, not only through the performance of the male voice choir but singing came quite spontaneously at weddings and funerals. A wedding reception could be quite an occasion, especially if the groom happened to play rugby and there was plenty of good beer. Soon one would hear the familiar Cornish songs, such as Trelawney, with a perfectly natural, balanced harmony. At a funeral one could often find that the church was well-filled, particularly if the deceased had connections with the sea. It could be very moving to listen to those male voices as they joined together in such hymns as, "Crossing the Bar".

On an occasion which had little to do with funerals or services in church, I was asked a question about this particular hymn. Returning one Wednesday morning after celebrating the Eucharist at St. Andrew's Church, I was passing the ice works when I heard a familiar voice, "Sir, I do want 'e for a minute or two." The voice was that of our Gwen, one of our truly interesting local characters. There she was in her apron and holding in her hand a rather large saucepan about to feed two swans which were waiting for her in the little pool that forms on the inside of the bridge. We exchanged a few pleasantries about the lovely day and then she asked her question.

"What's the first line of that hymn,'Crossing the Bar'?"

She explained that she had been singing the tune all the morning but could not for the life of her think how it began. I know the feeling, which can be most frustrating. Accepting the challenge, I began to oblige by singing the first verse:

Sunset and evening star,and one last call for me;
And let there be no weeping at the bar when I put
out to sea ...

It's Only the Vicar

I had got so far when Gwen joined in with a good strong voice, and only too glad to relieve her frustration.

We were quite enjoying our little duet when I noticed two ladies, obviously visitors, standing at the corner and listening to our little effort. As we came to the end of the verse one of them came forward, holding a coin in her hand, and asked quite sweetly, "Do we put the money in the saucepan?" Gwen's laughter could be heard all over Newlyn, "My handsome," she said, "You kin if you like but this is only the dress rehearsal."

Hymn singing played a great part in the life of the community and had special uses for particular occasions. Singing could take place out-of-doors as well as in homes or places of worship. One such use concerned the days of walking funerals. A certain name came up in conversation with the local doctor. He remarked, "Yes, he was a good man and was pitcher here for years."

I did not wish to display my ignorance. I could only think of 'pitcher' as describing either an earthenware vessel or perhaps the thrower in a game of baseball. Before we left I had to ask what was a pitcher. The explanation which proved so simple was readily forthcoming. After a funeral service in church or chapel the cortege would proceed up Paul Hill towards Paul Cemetery. Before the days of the motor-hearse that meant men either carried the coffin or pushed it along on a bier - quite an undertaking as those who know the road will appreciate. This involved having more than one team of bearers who would change over. Each time a change was made a fresh hymn would be sung and this is where our pitcher came in. It was his responsibility to pitch the tune in a key so that all could join in.

In those first years in Newlyn we had an almost full church for every funeral service. Today that is the exception rather than the rule. Very often there is just a few close friends and neighbours meeting with the family at the crematorium. This is particularly the case where some person, well-known and respected during their active life, has been out of circulation for some time before their death

New Parish

because of age, infirmity or a long illness. It is sad then to find a large church with less than a dozen people assembled to pay their respects.

As far as the Church of England is concerned those who are responsible for the finances, and particularly those who draw up the Table of Fees, must share some blame for this state of affairs. While there are many who can well afford to pay the funeral fees for the church service there are others who find this a real burden. In many cases where the funeral director informs the relatives what the fees will be for a church service, as compared with going to the crematorium or cemetery chapel, they opt for the cheapest and simplest way. This sometimes means that a faithful church family, because of poverty, go straight to the crematorium with no church service, while some wealthy people who have never darkened the church door ask for an elaborate church funeral service with the choir in attendance. In spite of this the clergy are constantly warned against making any exceptions or alterations in the fees laid down.

There is too such a difference in the way people react when there is a bereavement in the family. While there are some who are overwhelmed by the death of a near-relative, there are others who take it in their stride as a part of life, almost like an everyday occurence. Such indeed was the case of one particular parishioner in Newlyn.

Arriving home one evening at about five o'clock, after a day out of the parish, I entered the house to the sound of the telephone bell ringing. On lifting the receiver a voice immediately said, "Where have you been to all day sir?"

I recognised the voice, it was Bessie, a most likeable and colourful character who lived in the lodge of one of the distinguished local residences, and whose husband worked on the estate.

When I enquired if there were anything wrong I was told that Willie, her husband, 'had gone dead'. I at once expressed my concern and said that I was on my way to see her. On my arrival at the house I was taken to the bedroom and given a vivid description of how she had found him,

"There he was," she said, "Bottom up in the air, and the rest of him down between the bed and the wall."

On asking what practical measures still needed to be taken I was told that she must now get to Penzance to see to things. Since I, too, had to get to town for a meeting this was no problem and we were soon on our way. We were well on our way to our destination when Bessie called out for me to stop. "We have got to go right back again," she said. When I enquired the reason for this she replied, "It's the big football day tomorrow." I have to confess that I was completely confused by this reply and, when I asked for some clarification, she continued: "Willie's coupons are all done and there on the mantelpiece waiting to be posted."

Seeing no point in starting up a discussion, based on ethics, at this particular stage I turned about. I never heard of any winnings but, knowing what a kind and gentle person Willie had always been, I expect he was the winner in eternity while we were still the losers in time.

Newlyn

Visitors to Newlyn will recall the very fine building overlooking the harbour which houses the Royal National Mission to Deep-Sea Fishermen. During my time there it was restored at a cost of £52,000 - a considerable sum in those days. It was money well spent, for the mission renders a splendid service to fishermen and their families everywhere. Many people will be familiar with the service the Mission offers and which often features in the news when seamen are shipwrecked around the Cornish coast. The Mission has accommodation for sleeping and caring for men rescued from the sea.

The re-opening of the Mission after the restoration was a great day. There was much discussion at committee meetings to make it so.

There could be only one choice as to the opener. Colonel Sir Edward Bolitho, not only lived at nearby Trengwainton, but was a descendant of Nora Bolitho, who had given the building for the Mission in the first instance.

Sir Edward was a nonagenarian and a man of great stature in every respect. There was considerable debate as to how best to get him on to the platform but, on the day, all was well and he rose to the occasion superbly. His speech was delivered in a strong voice and with not a little eloquence.

However, when he caught sight of a certain Admiral on the platform, with whom he had had associations during the war, he departed from his well-prepared text and allowed

It's Only the Vicar

himself some reminiscence - and at some considerable length. He suddenly became aware of this and said, "It's time I sat down." He immediately did just that without, unfortunately, mentioning about the Mission being opened.

There followed some hasty whispering between officials on the platform and the message was delicately conveyed to Sir Edward. He insisted on getting to his feet again to finish the job, demanding considerable support on both port and starboard. With that the Mission was officially opened.

One pleasing association we had with the Mission was my discovery that the Superintendent had been a lay reader in a former Diocese and had a fine tenor voice. Accordingly he was soon involved in the life of St. Peter's and he went on from here to be ordained to the sacred ministry of the church. His experience gained with the R.N.M.D.S.F. must have proved invaluable to him in his pastoral work.

While the R.N.M.D.S.F. is fairly well known both nationally, and locally in Newlyn, few people realised that the Missions to Seamen also played a part in the life of Newlyn fishermen. Soon after my arrival I had a visit from a Mr. Brown, a retired fisherman who lived on the Gwavas Estate and was a keen member of Paul Church. He came to ask me to become the chaplain of the Fishermen's Rest. This meeting place comprised a large room in a building at the rise above the old quarry. Having gladly consented I was told when I would be expected to be there for my first service.

Brought up in the Church of England, my ideas about church services were, I suppose, rather limited and confined to liturgical forms to be found mainly in the Book of Common Prayer. Enquiring what was expected of me at the Fishermen's Rest I was told not to worry, we would sort it all out when I got there. And so it transpired. Not only did we sort it out when I got there but we more or less made it up as we went along! I always feel a little sad that one or two of these services were not recorded for posterity since they were quite unique.

Newlyn

Fortunately for me I knew the organist who performed on an old type of American Organ through meeting him at St. Andrew's Mission Church. Willie Mallon was a delightful person and, during the war years he had been a prisoner of the Japanese with Bishop Wilson, later Bishop of Birmingham. Like him, he had suffered considerably and was but a shadow of his former self when he was released. Added to this he now suffered from rheumatoid arthritis which became apparent during the first few bars of the first hymn.

"Oh dear!" Willie would remark when a discord was produced, "That won't do at all." He would manoeuvre into a more comfortable position then we could proceed. In fact, he was quite an accomplished organist. Naturally, it was to Willie that I looked for a little prompting as the service got under way. It all went something like this:

"Well," said the secretary, "It's about time we made a start, now what shall we have?" (That sort of remark in a place with the name "The Fishermen's Rest" could, of course, have had a different interpretation from the one intended here). But this reference was to the choice of the first hymn. There came a chorus of voices, "Better have number eighteen to get a good start."

Number eighteen in the Church Army hymn book, I was soon to discover from frequent repetition, was the stirring hymn, "Will your anchor hold in the storms of life?" We were soon singing it lustily with a good courage and, although some of the men had retired from the sea and were advancing in years, there were some fine voices among them. We came to the end of the last chorus and there was a slight pause and a knowing look from Willie Mallon to indicate that it was time for me to lead the prayers.

By this time I had got the gist of what was expected of me. I used extempore prayer, which I felt would be more fitting here and was pleased to find that, as I went along, there were murmurs of assent from the men, indicating how much they were sharing in the worship and the particular petitions. We concluded by saying together the Lord's

Prayer. Then one of the members asked, "Has brother Donald got a reading for us?" Donald at once produced his Bible and began to read in a good clear voice and with plenty of expression, while we all listened intently. The reading finished, someone asked, "What are we going to have now then?"

Someone piped up, "Let's have, 'What a Friend we have in Jesus'. That was Father Faull's favourite." (Father Faull was a saintly blind priest who once helped in the parish.) As we came to the end of this hymn it became abundantly clear to me what was to happen next.

"Now brothers," said Dick Simmonds, "I'm sure we are waiting to hear what message our new friend has brought for us tonight." Fortunately, again, I had considered this possibility and had given it some thought, and so my message for the men that evening was delivered in response to this invitation. There were various brief utterances from the assembled company as we went along. Thankfully, I discovered these were to support and to emphasise what I was saying. Then came the final hymn and prayers and there was plenty of time for informal talk and discussion - something I greatly valued. Before leaving I made enquiries about the time of our next service.

"Shall I come along next Tuesday at the same time?" I suggested.

"No, now wait a minute," I was told, "We had better look at the tide table." This invaluable record was duly consulted. "No, no good at all," came the reply. "That's neap tides then and we shall be fishing the Backs, better leave 'n for another fortnight now." I bowed to the providential ordering of the rise and fall of the tides.

I began to enjoy these services and getting to know these stalwart characters whose lives had been so much shaped by their close association with the sea. Nearly all of them had nick-names, and one was generally known as "The Colonel". He was the philosopher of the group and loved nothing better than a good argument. He was well read and had an up-to-date knowledge of what was going on in the world.

Newlyn

One particular notion, which he often voiced in those early days of my association with "The Rest", was his theory that this country would be far more prosperous and a better place to live in were it not burdened with a lot of old and decrepit people. He argued that every person on their seventieth birthday should be given a tablet which would quietly end their days on this earth.

"Think of all the trouble this would save," he would point out, "And everything would be organised, neat and tidy." "After all," he would conclude, "We've all had a very good innings by then".

When I had spent a year or two in their company I found that I knew these men quite well and was able to sense when anything was wrong. One evening I felt there was a certain atmosphere about the place the moment I entered and, as I was leaving I was accompanied up the slip by one of the men.

"Everything all right?" I asked.

"Well, to tell you the truth, there's nothing really wrong," came the reply, "Only 'tis the Colonel's seventieth birthday, and Cake asked him if he's taken his tablet yet or was he going to wait until he got home!" He continued "They were just having a few strong words when you happened to come in, but it will soon blow over." Indeed it did, and the subject was never mentioned again.

Cake was one of those kindly outspoken characters who could always be relied upon to say just the right thing. He was one of the crew of the *Rosebud* which sailed up the Channel and the Thames to Parliament to try to prevent the pulling down of many fishermen's cottages for road-widening. As they came in sight of the Houses of Parliament and Big Ben loomed before them, Cake pulled out his watch and remarked, "Damme, that one's wrong for a start."

These were fine men, not only deeply religious, but genuine and generous in their daily living and dealings with one another. On the way to a service at The Rest one evening I met the skipper of one of our local fishing boats. He was greatly upset because they had just lost one of his crew overboard; he had vanished without trace. It was his first trip back after a spell away from the sea. Donald related to me how they had gone below for a cup of coffee, but this good man had decided to stay on deck because his tummy was not quite used to things yet and he preferred to stay up in the air. "When we came up he had just disappeared," Donald told me. It was quite moving to hear how, in the midst of his deep concern for the crewman and his family, he excused his little fishing boat from any improper behaviour in a reasonable swell.

During that service we especially remembered all those who were involved, and not least the man's family. Next morning, quite early, the first of my callers arrived. It was Dick from The Rest with a £5 note, his own little contribution to the man's family. Quite a sum for a retired man living on his pension in those days. Such was the depth of feeling and fellowship among these men.

A year or two passed, and we continued to meet in our big room which was owned by a former Trinity House pilot. Unfortunately, some of the rent we paid him was spent all too quickly on drink, and it showed. Going down Market Jew Street in Penzance one Saturday afternoon following a wedding in St. Peter's Church, I found our good friend in the midst of an argument and quite prepared to take on anyone. Seeing that this might soon get out of hand, I suggested to him that, as I was going back to Newlyn, I might give him a lift home. After some slight resistance to the idea he finally agreed and scrambled into the seat of our old Humber Hawk beside me.

When we arrived back at Newlyn, however, my companion had decided that he was very comfortable where he was and made it plain that he was not going to shift for anybody or anything. Not wishing to land him at the vicarage in that condition, and equally not fancying an all-out struggle to unseat him, I had to think of some other solution.

Driving around to the Tolcarne Inn I drew up with his door right against the front door of the pub. It worked like magic. Without a word he immediately got out and by the

Newlyn

time he had staggered to the front door and found it was locked I was well on my way.

Not long after this we learned that we had to leave our familiar room as it was to be modernised as a cafe. I hasten to add that it had nothing to do with the little incident just recorded. There was now much speculation as to what should be done. We eventually decided to hold a meeting of all those interested with invitations to the Mayor of Penzance, Alderman Alfred Beckerleg, and certain Harbour Commissioners. The meeting was held at the end of November and it was resolved that we should aim to have some place we could call our own. The Harbour Commissioners kindly offered us a site on the Old Quay and the Mayor promised to send out an appeal to the borough.

At that time I had the honour of being the Mayor's Chaplain and it was no surprise to me to receive a telephone call from his office a day or two after our meeting. This was not, however, as I anticipated, to do with some future engagements but concerned the Fishermen's Rest. He had discovered that this was about the time when he sent out his Christmas appeal for the needy residents of the borough. In the light of this he asked me if the appeal could go out in my name rather than his. I readily agreed without realising how deeply this was to involve me. From this time forward I seemed to be landed with entire responsibility for this venture.

I sought the aid of one of the Harbour Commissioners, who was also a member of the town council, to keep an eye on the legal aspects and, in particular, any planning regulations. I was relieved and grateful when he agreed to help. A few weeks later, I was in St. John's Hall for a meeting of the town council and, after prayers, my good friend took me by the arm and said, "You know it's going to be all right for building that little Mission Room down on the Old Quay."

The very next day I conveyed this good news to the members and they were naturally delighted. We had already decided that this was to be a 'do-it-yourself' effort, and it was not more than a day or two before concrete blocks, sand and cement were arriving at the site and building was begun.

The manager of the Penlee Quarry, Mr.Mark Gooden, moored his boat nearby and seeing our efforts he generously arranged for two of his masons to come along and give a hand. Soon the walls had been built and, with the money which had now come in from the appeal, we were able to engage a local builder, Mr. Dennis Richards, to erect the roof. Never was a building run up with such speed, goodwill and enthusiasm!

Then came a rather nasty jolt to our enterprise. A very official looking envelope arrived through the post addressed to, "The Secretary, The Fishermen's Rest, Newlyn". It asked about planning permission.

We had gone ahead with the building simply on the friendly indication that there would be no problems, but now, some newly-elected members of the town council were asking questions about this building on an ancient monument and what planning permission had so far been given.

The fishermen were up in arms at the very thought that what we had so far accomplished might have to be torn down. It was arranged for the County Surveyor to pay a visit and see for himself what had been done. I could see a whole lot of trouble ahead if some of these older fishermen were there when he arrived. Gently I pointed out that the fault was ours, in fact I had to admit it was chiefly mine and, therefore, that I must accept the responsibility. Therefore it would be best if we met the surveyor, cap-in-hand, and be as nice as possible.

To this end I hand-picked a few who could be relied upon, including of course, our secretary, and then we held a little rehearsal of how we thought the meeting should go. When the time came all played their parts so well that it became all too obvious that we had resolved to co-operate to the full. We were getting, "Yes Sir," and "No Sir," before the good man had fully expressed what was in his mind.

Newlyn

Thankfully this official was kindly disposed towards fishermen in general and to the enterprise that we had shown and, in addition, had a sense of humour. He made various alterations in the way that we should finish the work to retain the appearance of an old fisherman's cottage which had been converted, and we readily agreed.

It still meant, however, that we had to go through all the motions and submit plans for every stage of the work. This meant I had to go and see a local architect. I told him about our proposal to build a Fishermen's Rest, and he was full of enthusiasm. He suggested that I should go away and think the matter over carefully, and then give him some ideas as to the number to be catered for, what amenities we planned, and so forth and he would draw up some provisional plans. He was slightly less enthusiastic when I told him that it would suit our purpose far better if he would be so kind as to go down to the Old Quay at Newlyn and draw just what he found standing there. He did see the lighter side of all this and kindly did the work for us without making any charge.

After all these ups and downs we eventually came to the opening of the new Fishermen's Rest; it turned out to be a memorable occasion. The Mayor, of course, was in attendance and made a speech. So too was the Revd. David Roberts, Chaplain to the Missions to Seamen, but what really stole the show were the lines of fishermen in their very best navy blue jerseys. The whole thing was rounded off with the ladies of the parish serving a splendid tea. Still in my possession and greatly valued, is an oil painting of the opening ceremony by Edna Bridge, one of the Newlyn artists. Evidently I was not going to be allowed to forget my foolish ways!

I sometimes look back on those days and wonder if I did right by continuing the informal way of worship that I found on my arrival. Would it not have been better to have advanced into a more dignified and set form which could have been followed from a book especially arranged?

Of one thing I feel sure, the act of worship in some great cathedral where a choir was singing something by

It's Only the Vicar

Bach, Byrd, Tallis or Handel could not have been heard more readily before the Throne of Grace than members of the Fishermen's Rest singing, "Will your anchor hold?" while Willie Mallon struggled with his arthritis at the American organ.

Day by Day

Looking back over past years it is so easy to think of the very special things that happened, and to lose sight of those everyday happenings which really make up life. In Newlyn, as in other parishes, it is the Daily Offices as well as the celebration of the Eucharist that lie at the heart of the Church's life. It was the custom to have services of Holy Communion during the week on various days in the early morning, and always on Festivals and Holy Days. There was also provision for the elderly in that, on certain Monday mornings at a later hour, there would be a service of Holy Communion in the St. Francis Chapel, often with the Laying on of Hands for the sick.

While Sunday was the great day for the whole parish at St. Peter's, it was the turn of St. Andrew's each Wednesday for the faithful to gather together. Holy Communion would be celebrated in the morning at 10 a.m. and Evensong would follow later in the day at 7 p.m. Invariably I walked to St. Andrew's, not only for the exercise, but also for the sheer joy of being able to speak to so many people on the way. Quite often, as I made my way home in the evenings the smaller boats would be landing their catch and I would be thrown a few mackerel, or whatever happened to be going. During all those years we were in Newlyn we were kept supplied with fresh fish through the wonderful generosity of the local people.

The longer I stayed, the more involved I became with the families that made up that community. The more involved I became, the greater the insight I had into the trials and sorrows that many of them had to bear. Some families were prone to every kind of sickness and disaster, and it was always especially sad when parents had to cope with the death of their children. Yet, because they had known hard times, they faced these crises with great courage and fortitude.

In a place the size of Newlyn one had to expect there would be many deaths among the ageing members of the town. However there were those tragic moments when those from the younger generations died, either from sickness or accident. A young wife died soon after her marriage from an attack of asthma leaving a distraught husband and her parents trying to cope with the situation. A father, with his young family still dependent on him, died while swimming in a local pool. I remember the parents of a lovely young girl of about eight who was killed on a pedestrian crossing.

At such times the parish priest becomes very much one of the family. You do not have to wait to be invited indoors - you are expected just to walk in and be there, whatever time of day or night. Cups of tea are poured out and put in front of you and all formalities are forgotten.

Even when there was no such tragedy or sickness, there was a wonderful freedom about the way I was received in the homes of these good people. Where else but in Newlyn would one be asked to "come in and speak to father" at 1 a.m.? Imagine my surprise in those early days to find that I was expected to go upstairs to see him, since he had already retired to bed, and hold a conversation for half-an-hour or so, with his good wife snoring away quite contentedly beside him!

Adversity and trials of various kinds have a way of breaking down barriers. Families who have been at variance for generations can be brought together again by some tragedy within the family. Not only this, it also has a way of bringing together those of different denominations within the Church so that they forget all their differences.

During the whole of the time I spent in Newlyn I had a

very happy relationship with the members of other churches and their ministers. It was expected of me that I should visit the sick regardless of any particular label he happened to wear. This was a great advantage and I personally received much help from those whom I visited, whether they were devout members of some church, or none but were, one often discovered, most grateful for any pastoral ministrations that one could offer.

One Methodist lady I frequently called on was a great inspiration to all of us who came to her home. She had been taken seriously ill not very long after her marriage. Now she lay quite helpless, looking for all the world like a very large doll in a box. She could not move at all and she was completely blind. Thankfully she could still hear and was able to speak in a very hoarse kind of voice. Her husband, too, was a wonderful person who nursed his wife with great care, ran the home and did a full-time job in an office. Here, too, we saw the Christian community at work as neighbours and friends popped in and out and saw to any particular needs that might arise through the day.

The most wonderful thing, perhaps, of all was that this dear Christian soul not only spent much time in prayer but, although apparently quite helpless, was able to raise a lot of money for charity. During her time of quiet she thought up ways of raising money for good causes. Then she would finance these projects and get her friends to carry them out on her behalf.

There was never a time when there were not some people from the parish in hospital. While some went to Truro, Tehidy, or even farther afield, the majority went to the West Cornwall Hospital. This meant that I became an almost daily visitor at the West Cornwall and, in consequence got to know the staff very well. One often hears complaints from clergy about the way they are received in hospitals or the way doctors stay quite aloof from them. Over the years I have learnt that it is all a question of getting to know one another and in so doing build up mutual confidence and trust. Certainly I found the greatest kindness and co-operation, not only from the hospital staff but also from the various doctors in general practice. Being on friendly terms with the hospital staff sometimes led to some unusual requests.

A certain retired schoolmaster found himself becoming a regular visitor at the hospital since his wife was there as a patient. After quite a long illness the lady died leaving a lonely and lost widower to try to fend for himself. During the time he was visiting the hospital, however, he had a great admiration for the staff in general and for one ward Sister in particular. This gratitude and admiration soon led on to other ideas. He confided to me one day that, while he felt very deeply about the lady in question, he did not know how to make the first move and, had I any suggestions? Since it was nearing Christmas time I suggested that he might go along to the ward and volunteer to help put up the decorations. I did add there was always the possibility that a pair of steps might slip and he could find himself in a hospital bed which would afford him ample time to make his feelings known to the unsuspecting Sister!

Before this plan could be put into operation he telephoned me with a request that I should take her a box of chocolates as a little present from him. Providence then took a hand for, as he came out of the shop holding this offering of such consequence, he quite literally bumped into the lady for whom it was intended. Whether it was the shock of this happening or not we shall never know, but the ice was broken and he immediately invited her to take coffee with him. The invitation was accepted and the box of chocolates there and then presented. It was therefore, no surprise to me when they called at the vicarage together to make arrangements for their marriage. Another patient who stands out in my memory, since he found himself in hospital at that time, was a young schoolboy by the name of Gareth. He was a lively lad who could always be counted on to be up to something. At this particular time he and one of his mates were playing at jumping on and off the pavement during a busy time in the town. Gareth had chosen the wrong moment to jump out in front of a milk lorry which went over him, causing terrible injuries.

Day by Day

A phone call from the hospital with the news that he had been knocked down by a lorry took me there hoping that it was nothing more than a broken leg or arm. On arrival I saw his mother sitting anxiously in the corridor and, just at that moment saw Gareth being wheeled towards the children's ward.

"It may not be too bad," I said to the mother, "At least they are not whisking him away to another hospital." How wrong I was. When I spoke to Matron, who was bringing up the rear of the little procession as they entered the ward, she explained to me that things could hardly be worse. There were various internal injuries which were bleeding and besides this (their chief concern at that moment), there were multiple fractures. One tried to convey this information to the mother without shattering her hopes and at the same time conveying the seriousness of the situation.

That evening Gareth's own doctor told me that he had just taken another look at the boy and then gone off to say his prayers. He did, however, add that the surgeon was going to perform an emergency operation to deal with the internal bleeding. This operation was successful but the poor lad was still in a critical condition.

It was wonderful the way the hospital responded to all this. To avoid moving Gareth to an orthopaedic hospital at this stage there was a lot of improvisation to deal with the fractures and, with many ups and downs, he gradually pulled through. Never have I seen more courage and determination, with not a word to express any pain or discomfort. It was not very long before we saw that daring side of Gareth reappearing. Going into the ward one afternoon I noticed the curtains around his bed had been drawn and my heart sank.

"Nothing to worry about as far as he's concerned," said the Sister, "That's only for our protection."

It appeared that, with the tiny movement he had recovered in one hand, our Gareth had projected some missile which had struck another boy with considerable force just below the eye, leaving some painful evidence.

When Gareth was eventually discharged from hospital,

still very much encased in plaster, we were having a new bell put into St. Peter's turret. Various ladders were left in place over-night with planks lashed to them to deter any would-be adventurers. Imagine my concern and surprise one morning when I spied Gareth at the very top of those ladders, plaster and all. "I was just coming up to see you Vicar," he explained, "And then I thought I would just pop up here to see how they are getting on."

Not all young people are as fortunate as Gareth, who was blessed with having good parents and a pretty young sister. Young Billie was not so fortunate. He was then only about two or three years of age and not expected to live. That particular evening I had rather a tight programme, having to take Evensong at 7 p.m. and then get back to St. Peter's Church Hall to be made up to take part in one of the plays running at that time.

Just before the service at St. Andrew's was over I was handed a brief note which asked that I should go at once to the hospital for an emergency baptism. Taking a surplice and stole I hastened on my way and as I got near to the hospital remembered that, in my haste, I had brought no prayer book. At the same moment I remembered that I had been given a Book of Common Prayer by an old lady to place in the church. It was still in the pocket of the car. I took it and with confidence restored I went into the ward. There the Home Sister had everything beautifully prepared, and the nursing staff were standing around the little bed.

If you are familiar with some of the older prayer books, you may know that what are sometimes called "The Occasional Offices" are in very small print. I found that, in the subdued lighting I just could not read a thing. It was one of those moments when you stay quiet and ask for silent prayer to be joined with yours, hoping that at the end of that time words would come flooding back to memory. In due course they did, once the first few words had arrived the rest just followed, and it was a very moving time for all of us as young Billie was baptised and made a member of Christ, the child of God and an inheritor of the Kingdom of Heaven.

Day by Day

We said some prayers for his recovery, and for the young mother who was with us in a distressed state.

Expressing my gratitude to the staff I went out, made my way hurriedly to the church hall to take my part in the play with a lot still on my mind. The young boy whom I had baptised had been the victim of his father's brutality. He had beaten him and flung him down some granite steps. The boy was hardly expected to live through the night and I felt that, as soon as possible, I should go to see the father who was in police custody.

It is usual at such times for a parent to be filled with remorse and almost in despair. In fact, most men who find themselves in a police cell come to their senses and are only too willing to talk and co-operate. As soon as it was possible, that evening, I went along to see this man. To my surprise he was arrogant and as unrepentant as any person I have met. When I told him I had baptised Billie, he took me to task and asked what right I had to baptise his son. His mention of rights was a favourable opening for me to say a few words on this subject, and what is right and what is not right for any man. Thankfully the child lived through all this, but was in some respects handicapped for the rest of his life.

Fortunately all such ministrations do not have to be carried out in such circumstances nor in such a hurried manner. Some pastoral work, by its very nature, needs to be conducted in an atmosphere of calm with no sense of hurry at all. Such was indeed the case of a lady who lived on the outskirts of Newlyn in a delightful bungalow at Tredavoe. Since her husband had died she seemed to be under considerable stress and was not really herself. Things became so difficult that her doctor suggested that, if I really had time, and could get her talking, then she might improve and so do without the necessity of sending her away for treatment.

Choosing my time carefully I made my way to see this good lady one afternoon when I judged she would have just completed her afternoon rest. All this went according to plan and I was greeted by this charming and gentle lady as I

It's Only the Vicar

went up the path to her front door. What, however, I had not allowed for was her little dachsund, three years of age and having the name of Dennis.

Dennis was extremely jealous of his owner and most protective. In consequence he kept circling me at great speed using every opportunity to nip at the bottoms of my trousers. My plans for a calm and relaxed atmosphere were fast falling apart. My opportunity came as I sank into a low arm-chair and my opponent came around from behind. Reaching out my hand, and unseen by my hostess, I grabbed his collar and made sure I had a firm grip. It worked like a charm. Dennis immediately settled down and, during the whole of the time we were talking I could feel him breathing gently up the sleeve of my coat. I began to reproach myself for the rather harsh thoughts I had entertained about this little dog on my arrival and to feel grateful that his mistress and I could talk in peace - not even a bark or growl.

The time came for us to draw our conversation to an end and I promised to call again. Imagine my surprise when I got up from my chair to find that my coat sleeve was hanging down from the elbow in two rather jagged strips. During the whole time I had imagined that Dennis was almost asleep, he had been busy chewing his way up my sleeve. I covered it all up as best I could and went unnoticed as far as the change in my apparel was concerned. My journeys to this little bungalow at Tredavoe became quite frequent from that day, and I am glad to record that Dennis and I had gained a certain mutual respect, and we certainly kept our distance.

Mental illness is always a great problem and can be as distressing for relatives as for the patient. I was struck by the number of people with fairly mild mental disorders who were cared for by their families without ever a thought that they should be put into any form of institution. Some of these might be described as just eccentric. Into this category we should perhaps put our dear Janie, who lived over in the Bowjey area. Like Anna in the New Testament she spent her time in the house of the Lord, which for Janie

Wolf lighthouse

Sevenstones lightship

The Author as Rector of St Mawgan

Newlyn St Peter Centenary with Bishop Maurice Key

Day by day

meant either St. Peter's or St. Andrew's. There she would be found at prayer or reading her Bible. She also took part in the Daily Offices, making her feeble responses and reading her part in the Psalms with some difficulty. Janie was a familiar figure going through the streets of Newlyn with her bag containing food for "her" birds which flocked around her as she fed them outside St. Peter's Church.

Never did she find a word to speak against any person or thing. To say that the weather was bad would bring a mild rebuke from her who saw everything around her as perfect beauty. Often she would talk about her father who had worked with the Missions to Seamen and owned a little boat called 'The Dayspring'. Janie, though so gentle, could be very set in her ways and would hold out with great determination. Once, when we were putting in a new ceiling at St. Andrew's Church, we had arranged to have the celebration of Holy Communion in the little crypt below. This would not satisfy Janie who insisted that Holy Communion must always be in "the Upper Room", whatever the circumstances. She absolutely refused to join us in the crypt, which was really a delightful little chapel and just right for small gatherings.

As she got older, Janie became more and more frail, and that meant I had to collect her in the car if she were to get to church at all. It also became obvious that she was not feeding herself properly and, in addition to all this we had noticed a rodent ulcer appearing beneath one eye. In spite of all the efforts which were made by the out-patient sister at the hospital, who happened to live quite near, and myself, she resolutely refused to see a doctor or have any form of treatment other than that which she administered herself. This consisted in bathing it with warm water. With this as the only attention it received, it gradually grew worse and worse. It must have proved very distressing for her - though she would never mention it.

When she was no longer able to get about except with great difficulty, she allowed me to visit her home with her Communion. It was then I began to see how bad things really were and got the help and co-operation of her sister-in-law. Janie was living on nothing but bread and milk. Even a tin of Ovaltine which I had managed to leave with her was not touched and had been wrapped up to return to me. In the circumstances I was in touch with the health authorities to ask them to call.

They explained that a Health Visitor had tried to call on various occasions without being able to gain entry. I assured them that if a doctor would give us a time, Janie's sister-in-law and myself would be there to let him in. This was soon arranged and it was not long after the doctor had seen her that an ambulance was on its way. As I helped to carry her out on a stretcher, (not a very heavy task), she looked up at me and said, "I will forgive you for all this, and hope that in time the Lord will too."

They worked wonders with her at the hospital. An operation was necessary to remove the eye and much of the area that had become affected and at last they were able to get some nourishing food inside her. A typically Irish sister told me how. She went along to Janie with her evening meal of soup and she told her to take it away since the good Lord had said she must have nothing but bread and milk. "Now, and there's a funny thing," came the prompt reply. "The good Lord has just this minute been having a word with me and said that this is what I must bring ye."

As time has gone on I have sensed a certain change in the work of the Sacred Ministry as it affects parish life. Fewer clergy has meant the emergence of "group" or "team" ministries and the uniting of benefices. The greatest loss here is time for regular pastoral visiting in the parish. I wonder if this need be the case. Though circumstances change I have found it still possible to keep to a rule I set myself long ago, to be in not less than thirty different homes each week, in addition to an almost daily hospital visit.

One of the things that bedevils many clergy today and this certainly includes most of our bishops, is the ever-increasing number of meetings, district church councils, parochial church councils, endless committees, synod

Day by day

meetings at different levels, working parties and commissions. Surely we are getting things the wrong way round. If the work were carried out in the parishes as it should be, there would be no need for about half these get-togethers, which for my part I have almost invariably found depressing, to say the least.

Each incumbent of a parish will have his own particular gifts and talents to offer. These can vary considerably, and therefore one must never try to make comparisons. I was fortunate to enter a line of faithful parish priests at Newlyn and each had given generously of their various attributes. Among them there were scholars, artists and at least one who was something of a pioneer in the local fishing industry.

My immediate predecessor, Fr. Jim Maddock, had been a faithful and hard-working parish priest, and his ministry was still very much appreciated during my time. He was especially remembered for his constant visiting throughout the parish. The third incumbent was the Rev. John Pope Vibert who, besides being vicar, took a lively interest in the fishing industry and was one of those instrumental in getting the erection of the new pier under way. He was followed by the scholarly Fr. Lach-Szyrma who was also tireless in his work among the fishing community.

Another priest who left his mark was Fr. Alan Wyon. As a boy I can remember him as the curate at Saltash before he took the living of Newlyn. By then he had already established himself as a sculptor well-known for his artistry and skill. He used these special gifts to enrich and beautify the church of Newlyn St. Peter during the time he served there as Vicar from 1936-1955. He carved the large crucifix above the altar and set it beneath its rich canopy of gold and red. Immediately over the altar he placed a high-relief of the Last Supper, after Leonardo da Vinci. This has been tastefully coloured by his wife who was well-known in the world of art. Undoubtedly, however, Fr. Wyon will be best remembered for his life-size bust of the Madonna and Child. Executed in marble, it has about it a sense of

It's Only the Vicar

purity and tranquility which makes a lasting impression on all who have had the privilege of seeing it over the years.

When I arrived in Newlyn, quite a number of people asked me if I painted. I had to confess that my painting was limited to about once a year in the Spring with a six inch brush and a bucket of emulsion. It soon became obvious that this rather mundane talent that had been given me might be used to good effect inside St. Peter's since the walls and ceiling were peeling off and had become discoloured with mould and dust. We decided that much of this work of restoration could be done by volunteers, although we thought it advisable to make a local contractor responsible for the interior of the roof. This required scaffolding and many days of preparation before any painting could be begun.

There was a splendid response to our appeal for help. Coming into the church one evening and hearing a call from the east end I beheld the Commander of Trinity House Vessel *Stella* standing on the edge of the red and gold canopy and delighted that he had discovered a stained glass window hidden behind it. I could only stand in amazement, not at the fact that a window had been discovered, but the fact that the whole thing did not come crashing to the ground. This canopy consisted of little more than pressed paper mounted on some very slender battens, and the figure standing triumphantly upon it could hardly have been less than 14 stone. A verse from the Psalms came to mind; "He shall give his angels charge over thee: and in their hands they shall bear thee up ..." It seemed the only explanation at the time.

However, we were not so fortunate a little while after this when some patching up had to be done. Sea-sand had been used in the plaster so there was the occasional patch which showed some activity and needed attention. One evening a few of us had assembled to make good some of these defects. We could deal with most of the problems but some concern was being expressed as to how we should cope with an area way up in the apex above the Lady Chapel.

Day by day

Someone then volunteered that this could safely be left with Mr. Harry Bounden who would be along later. Harry was indeed a professional, tall, agile and always willing. Sure enough, he turned up with his huge brush tucked beneath his belt. Without a moment's hesitation he was ready to tackle the bit that all the rest of us had been only too willing to leave to him. With a large bucket of white emulsion paint he was soon up the extension ladder and working away. Seeing the ladder was resting on polished tiles I offered my services to stand at the bottom.

"Don't waste time doing that," said Harry, "Take a brush and a pair of steps and paint up so far to meet me."

I readily and obediently complied. I was just going to dip my brush in the bucket when there was a terrific crash. In that split second Harry had come down, crushing my steps as he passed by. There he lay, flat on the tiles, while every terrible consequence flashed through my mind. It was a relief when he stirred and was able to get up. Thank heavens he was so fit, and although he suffered some grazing and bruising, was not seriously injured, and no bones broken.

During the whole of this episode his wife had been engaged in wiping off any odd spots of paint that appeared on the floor. At the sight of her unfortunate husband, she passed out and one or two of us then turned our attention to bringing her around. As she regained consciousness she looked up at me and asked, "Are you going to play cricket Vicar?" Not until that moment was I really aware that I had been the sole beneficiary of Harry's bucket of emulsion paint. I made my way to the back lawn of the vicarage where I divested myself of my clothes and went in search of a bath.

In the midst of all our enthusiasm to have St. Peter's looking bright and clean inside, we did not overlook St. Andrew's. To overcome the problem of loose plaster falling from the ceiling, we engaged Mr. Nicky Peake, a local boat-builder, to erect a lower ceiling giving the effect of a barrel-roof, and making the place much warmer, as well as a lot cleaner.

It's Only the Vicar

A few enthusiasts, including some of the younger generation, assembled during the evening to brighten up the interior. To crown our efforts Mr. & Mrs. Tudor, of Penzance School of Art presented St. Andrew's with a series of painted panels to go behind the Font, as well as a large and beautiful piece of embroidery depicting a dove, representing the Holy Spirit, to hang over the Font.

This was such a beautiful work that I was naturally thrilled to see it in that delightful little church with its open stone work and simplicity of style, and many people came to admire what had been done. I was slightly taken back, however, when one of the older ladies of the congregation stood looking intently up at it. "What's it supposed to be?" she enquired. I explained that it depicted a dove hovering, which represented, according to ancient tradition, the Holy Spirit. "Dove!" she remarked, "I thought 'twas a great seagull."

It would hardly be possible to enumerate all those characters who had been so tremendously helpful to me during my ministry in Newlyn. I am not thinking only of those directly concerned with the Parish Church of Newlyn St. Peter. Many of those gave splendidly and sacrificially of their time and talents. But there was also a whole variety of people in all walks of life who gave me such a welcome amount of help and encouragement. The matron and staff of the West Cornwall Hospital were always most co-operative during my visits, whatever time of day or night.

I remember too, how the almoner at that time, Miss Nixon, could always put her finger on the very thing that would provide the answer to some problem. Once in a conversation, I happened to speak of the plight of the mother of two lovely girls who was married to one of our local fishermen. She was a native of Greece and had married this particular Cornishman at 16 when he was serving with the British Army. She was now terribly homesick and, although she was promised time and again she would be able to go home and visit her people, when the time came there was never enough money. Because of this continued frustration she was now at breaking point.

Day by day

Immediately Miss Nixon enquired whether I had been in touch with the Hellenic Association and I had to confess that I had not even heard of such a body. She produced the address, and another apparently insoluble problem was well on its way to being solved. Doctors in the area, too, were always most helpful and ready to show special concern for any that I happened to bring to their attention.

One delightful character who was always something of an inspiration was Father Edgar Faull, a blind priest being cared for at the Home of the Epiphany at St. Agnes. He had at one time worked in Newlyn and still loved nothing better than to be brought over to his old parish for a day to visit many of those whom he still remembered.

It was quite an experience to walk dear old Fr. Faull around Newlyn for, as we walked along, people would recognize him and greet him most warmly. Not once do I remember him being unable to identify the person who spoke to him and call them by name. One house in particular he used to call on was in Tredavoe Lane where two ageing sisters lived. They would talk animatedly about old times and then, just before he left they would ask him to pray with them and give them his blessing.

Another port of call would inevitably be at the Fishermen's Rest where the men truly loved him. Very often when I was there for a service someone would request Fr. Faull's hymn - 'What a Friend we have in Jesus ...' showing that they often had this saintly soul in mind.

At this time we had a blind chorister at St. Peter's by the name of Reg Hitchens. He was a piano tuner by profession and, not only did he play the piano, but he had a splendid tenor voice. One Sunday morning when Reg was in the choir, I was surprised to see a blind lady from my old parish of St. Mawgan, a Miss Audrey Hambly. I knew her well, she sang in our choir, and I often called at her home. When I enquired as to what brought Audrey to Newlyn I was told, in a slightly coy manner, that she had come to see a friend. The friend turned out to be Reg whom she had met at Malabar, the home for the blind in Truro, where they had sung a duet together to entertain the residents. From singing this duet together a romance had begun and was now truly blossoming, and I was delighted when, just a short time later they came to see me about getting married in St. Peter's Church.

When we started to speak of wedding arrangements, one person came immediately to mind - Fr. Edgar Faull. He happened to be a friend of Reg and I suggested that he should take part in the service. It was a moving occasion as Reg and Audrey stood before the old blind priest at this very special moment in their lives and he recited part of the service without once faltering over the words.

It continued to be a great joy to me to visit Reg and Audrey, and I was often able to meet them off the bus at Newlyn Bridge and bring them to church for Evensong. I remember one cold winter's evening, Reg remarking, "We won't be able to sing much tonight unless the words are familiar, it's far too cold." I must confess that I was completely puzzled by this statement at the time, but, when I started putting out their large volumes of the braille version of Hymns Ancient and Modern, I grasped what he was meaning. How can you possibly identify and follow the dots embossed on the paper if your fingers are numbed!

Reg and Audrey had their problems like everyone else, yet I never remember anything but happiness in their home. My memory is of Reg playing the piano or listening to some good music on the radio, and Audrey, if she were not singing, filling the whole house with her laughter.

Thank God for such people who help to point the way to true happiness.

Getting Organized

In the far West of Cornwall in the early 1960s people still liked to create their own entertainment. Penzance had choral, orchestral and dramatic societies of some distinction. In Newlyn we contented ourselves with the more homely organizations, many of which were connected with St. Peter's Church. For my part I found that my little bit of drama could come quite unexpectedly when I was about my normal actitities as a pastor visiting his people. There were constant surprises that had to be accepted without any sign of shock or emotion for the sake of those around. One such occasion stands out. I had been asked to visit a family because there had been a death in the household. Television was, just then, very much a novelty and I arrived at the house to find that while the death had occurred within the past hour or two, the family, with a few friends and neighbours, were still watching a programme on TV. The only light in the stuffy room came from the flickering of a television set. Being asked to take a seat and, not knowing where in the rather crowded room, I eventually perched myself on the end of one of those dual purpose settee come put-you-up arrangements. I knew, from previous experience, that some areas of this particular piece of furniture were not very comfortable, to say the least. I sat for about five minutes, hoping that the programme would soon be switched off and that I could talk to the family. Then, feeling somewhat uncomfortable,

It's Only the Vicar

I decided to change my posture slightly. Imagine my surprise when, on reaching out my hand to support myself, I found that I was holding the feet of the deceased and I was actually sitting on his legs.

This, it has to be admitted, was an exceptional case of addiction to "the box". In spite of all the competition from TV, however, the various organizations connected with the Church continued to flourish.

The Mothers' Union was looked after by a quiet, conscientious and most efficient Enrolling Member. We are grateful for what she did in keeping this large organization running smoothly and happily, and being very lively in all its activities within the parish. Not, mind you, that the M.U. Branch was at all stiff and starchy or conformed to the popular image. Some of them may have been advancing in years, and a few figures may have grown a bit wide in the beam, but they were all young at heart. When they appeared on the stage they could really let their hair down and kick their heels up. Some of their sketches could well have been shown in the West End.

At the other end of the scale there was an active branch of the Girls' Friendly Society. This valuable youth work had been running in the parish for some generations and, for much of that time had been under the guidance of the Sisters from the Community of the Epiphany. During my time, Sister Alice was with us and did a lot of work organizing weekly meetings, special services and the inevitable outings by coach for rallies and other special occasions.

One of the difficulties faced by Sister Alice on such outings was that some girls suffered from coach sickness. Nothing daunted, Sister Alice would set off armed with a good supply of plastic bags. Unfortunately this method of dealing with the problem tended to have a chain reaction and it was not unknown for half the company to be feeling queer, even though they managed to contain themselves until the journey's end.

Certain good ladies in the parish were of the greatest help in keeping this movement alive, among them were

Getting Organised

three sisters, the Misses Suzanne, Betty and Kitty Humphreys. They were ably backed up by Miss Joan Collins, who lived just across the road from the hall and Miss Alice Bennetto, ever ready to oblige on the piano.

For the younger lads we formed a company of the Church Lads' Brigade. Many people said that boys would not join a uniformed organization where there was emphasis on physical training, drill and discipline. Surprisingly the lads valued the discipline and were quite proud to be seen in their smart uniform.

We have already spoken of young Gareth and it was his father who became the C.O. of the company, ably supported by one of our local police constables. Also among the officers was Mr. Willie Uren who could always be counted on to be active in anything connected with church life. One of my little contributions was to coach them at cricket. Seeing one lad keeping wicket without very much idea as to why he was there, I asked him to stand to one side and watch me. "I'll show you how to do it," were my famous last words. Down came the ball, missing the bat the leg side. I dived, caught the ball and there was a loud crack - I had broken my arm! "That's the way to do it Vicar," was a cry often heard among the ranks after that day.

By far the largest group of young people connected with the Church comprised the open Youth Club, which met on Saturday evenings. These were the days when discos were just beginning and many evenings were devoted to this kind of activity. I am for ever grateful to those gallant people connected with the Church who gave up so much time and energy to running this, the most difficult group of all. We had stalwarts like John Page, for many years editor of "The Cornishman", Beth Green, a schoolteacher, Jim Harman and his wife Elizabeth, and many more. I must confess that, but for their loyal support I could not have faced each Saturday evening and, even then I heaved a sigh of relief when the last of the youngsters had gone home and the hall had been cleaned up ready for Sunday School the next day.

It's Only the Vicar

One evening I did go a bit early when all seemed to be winding up in the normal way. Just as I was getting into bed there was a sustained ringing of the door-bell. Evette had arrived to tell me that there was a fight on in the hall and one of our lads was bleeding badly.

Unfortunately, just as they were preparing to leave, some young men from outside the parish, who were obviously the worse for drink, pushed their way in and started this fight with some of our youngsters who were hardly mature enough for this kind of thing. To cool the situation I sent our young people quickly on their way home. They all went except a young man by the name of Chris Hill who absolutely refused to leave me on my own. Chris was a fine young man with a great sense of humour, as well as of loyalty. Tragically he was killed in a motor-cycle accident not long afterwards.

With Chris's support I tried to impress on the three intruders remaining that this sort of behaviour would not pay in Newlyn and, since I knew that the police had been called, I felt it right to detain them until these officers of the law arrived. It was something of a relief when John Page arrived together with our local policeman already well-known in Newlyn as a keeper of the peace. He dealt with this situation to such good effect that we were not troubled by this kind of behaviour again.

We found the police a great help in running this kind of open youth club, and occasionally Chief Inspector Jenkin would drop in for a talk with these youngsters. I can think of no other person who could grip the attention of this vigorous group of young people as he could; it was partly his personality and partly that he had obviously given a great deal of thought to it all before he arrived. He had a knack of knowing just how to hold their attention by switching from one topic to another at the right moment. Just as they were getting restless about hearing about the role of the police in general terms he would produce a lot of photographs from his pocket of recent accidents and say, "Any of you lads recognize this?" Immediately there would be renewed interest and, just as they were tiring of this he

Getting Organised

would ask if they had heard about a bit of smuggling that had been going on in the harbour. Always he would be driving home some special lesson.

I often wondered in those days if we were doing any good running this kind of open youth club. Often I felt that the tail was wagging the dog and that we were having little influence for good although, as many people would say, we were keeping the young people off the streets. Vindication came some years later. Not long before I left Redruth, I happened to be walking home from St. Euny Church and noticed on the opposite side of the road a car just drawing up. A well-dressed young gentleman got out, and, accompanied by two attractive teenage children, came across the road to speak to me. My first reaction was that here was someone who was going to enquire the way. He did not speak to me but addressed himself to his offspring and said, "Now this is the man I have often spoken to you about, who used to open up his chuch hall for us in Newlyn. I don't know how he put up with us lot in those days but he did more good than he'll ever know."

A chapter on parish organizations and activities would not be complete without some mention of St. Peter's Players, I am glad to note they are still in existence and doing well. It all started with a Christmas play performed in the hall because we felt this was more suitable than performing it in St. Peter's Church. This play proved to have such an appeal in Newlyn, and the performers found such pleasure in working together, that it was decided to carry on and do another play. This time something more secular was chosen. "Haul For The Shore" could not have been more apt, since the whole action is set in a fishing community very similar to that of Newlyn.

The Players were not confined to St. Peter's Church and this was a good thing. We were joined by friends from the Methodist Church and from the neighbouring Parish of St. Mary's Penzance. The Superintendent at the R.N.M.D.S.F. played the part of the vicar in the Play, a role that he was soon to play in real life. I was given the part of Petroc Pook and I was able to borrow from my friends at the Fishermen's Rest, not only their fishing boots and jersey but also some of their dialect and mannerisms. The first performance was a great occasion and we invited the members of the Fishermen's Rest to come along as our special guests. They greatly enjoyed their evening, but I was a little taken aback when they told me they thoroughly enjoyed it and the best part of the evening was the cup of tea during the interval.

So the St. Peter's Players came into being and staged more and more ambitious productions. It became apparent in some quarters that I was not remembering my lines as well as I might, a fact that was conveyed to me through my daughter who had now joined the little company. One actress, in particular, used to tell Ruth that she got all strung up if she had to follow me at any time because she never knew quite what kind of improvisation she would have to adapt to. Because of this and because the productions were mostly staged just as Lent was about to begin, I gradually withdrew from acting. That must have caused much relief in some quarters.

My last appearance was quite accidental in every sense of that word. The play in question was "Brides of March", a rather wild and hilarious production in which originally I had no intention of being involved at all. Just as the final rehearsals were about to begin there was a misfortune. Brian, who was taking the leading role met with a motor-cycle accident and broke his leg. I heard about this one afternoon, so it was no great surprise to find the producer and one or two others in the play on the door-step in the evening. Without giving them an opportunity to speak I said, "The answer is one big emphatic, NO." They were not to be put off so easily and asked me to hear what they had to say. Their request sounded quite simple: the producer would take Brian's place, and all that was asked of me was to appear at the end of the last scene. I didn't even have any lines to learn - just a little lively action was all that was needed.

It seemed quite impossible in these circumstances to refuse, seeing that I had the success of what they were

Getting Organised

doing very much at heart. The result can best be summed up by quoting the reaction of one of the old ladies who then lived in the Tolcarne area; "'Tis comin to a pretty pass up there, now with they St. Peter's Players, wot with the Vicar chasin a lot of naked maids around the stage."

There was one other organization that made a very valuable contribution to the parish without many people being very much aware of its existence. This was our branch of the Guild of St. Raphael which continued to meet regularly for intercession for the sick, as well as promoting the use of the Sacraments for the healing ministry. One great advantage in Newlyn was that quite a number of the medical profession lent their support. This kept the balance right and helped towards a better understanding of the needs of many people.

For a long time now, the Church of England has officially said that the Church should be concerned with the Ministry of Healing, and this has been made clear at successive Lambeth Conferences. However there still seems to be a reluctance on the part of many bishops to give clear and decisive leads to the clergy in this aspect of the Church's life. One can understand that there is always a fear at the back of their minds that things might get out of hand and that they could find themselves on the wrong side of the medical profession.

There has been a danger in some quarters for clergy and ministers to look upon the Church's role as being 'instead of' medical science rather than a means of co-operating and working beside the medical profession. This wrong approach has often led to claims being made for miraculous cures and, quite understandably, has tended to alienate doctors and nurses from what the Church is doing. I would not deny for one moment that there were cases in Newlyn where sick persons received great benefit from the Laying on of Hands, Holy Unction and the regular receiving of Holy Communion. I would regard this as a cause for thanksgiving among those concerned, but never as events to be publicised. Again and again we have had to learn more ourselves about the nature of God's healing, which did not always mean that a person was physically restored.

We had an example of this when a senior member of nursing staff became ill and had to stop work. She became the most difficult of patients. Restless and aggressive she could only talk about when she could get back to work and what was going on at the hospital while she was away. It soon became obvious that, far from getting better, she was gradually becoming more seriously ill, and it was at this stage that her mother asked that she be anointed.

A lot of preparation was made for this, not only with her but by a constant prayer among all members of the Guild. After she had received Holy Unction she continued to decline physically, but she was completely transformed as a person. She was so grateful for every little thing that was done for her and was obviously at great peace within her whole personality. Who would question for one moment that this was the form of healing that is far better and far more lasting than any other?

In this chapter we have taken a brief look at some of the various organizations within the parish, and one will have gathered that they played a very important part in meeting the needs of different groups of people. There are still some that I have not mentioned such as the Ladies' Fellowship, a group brought into existence to complement the work of the Mothers' Union. There were quite a number of ladies who felt the need of some social life within the Church yet did not fit into the programme followed by the M.U. For example many mothers with young children found it almost impossible to get to afternoon meetings, and the same applied to working wives. The great thing was that they all realised that they were only one part of the Church and that they still needed to worship and work together as a whole, as well as being able to pursue their own special interests.

Our Church Lads' Brigade never managed to hit the headlines as far as cricket was concerned, in spite of my "sacrifice". However we did manage to play one memorable friendly match. Since my arm had now mended

Getting Organised

the Lads agreed that I should be wicket-keeper on this occasion. It became obvious to me that every time the ball came down towards me and I crouched behind the wicket, peals of laughter came from the spectators behind me. This went on for several overs and those who were behind me at the batsman's end took up the chorus at every delivery.

As we changed ends once more, one of our senior boys came up to me with a certain amount of embarrassment and said, "I'm sorry to have to tell you this, Vicar, but I think we ought to change places and you could try your hand at bowling because your trousers are split right up the back."

A Feel of the Sea

It surprised me how quickly the first year in Newlyn passed by. I had arrived just after Easter in 1961, and, all too soon I found that I was preparing for my first season of Lent in the new parish. What I did not realise at that moment was the fact that it was to have a really dramatic start.

On the morning of Ash Wednesday, 1962, I was on my way to St. Peter's Church just after 6.30 a.m. for the first service of Holy Communion on the first day of Lent, when I met John Page. At that time he lived just opposite the church in Newlyn Coombe. He told me that the storm, which was still raging, had breached the sea walls and all the lower part of Newlyn was now flooded. With characteristic concern John had already been to see where help was needed and directed me to the Tolcarne area where there was already considerable distress.

As I went down the Coombe it registered with me that the stream, which I had always seen flowing down towards the sea, was now coming up to meet me. This was an early indication of the height of the tide at that moment, even so I had little idea of the sight that was to meet me at the sea front. Everywhere was awash with the waves pounding over the quay area and the tops of the waves and the spray going over the roofs of the houses.

The first house that I went to was that of Bobby Bean, a very sick man who lay paralysed in a downstairs room. Going inside the poor man's room I found that the water

A Feel of the Sea

was already knee-high, soaking the bed-clothes, while the waves were still pounding against the shutters which had been erected outside. I can still remember pulling the curtains across to give it a more comfortable feeling before sitting on his bed to give some assurance and the promise of help very soon.

We had not long to wait before Chief Inspector Jenkin arrived, a serene figure who was able to inspire confidence on every occasion. He at once ordered an ambulance which, fortunately was soon in the vicinity. Gaining access to the front of the house was impossible, the best that could be done was to approach down the back lane. Gently, poor Bobby was carried to the waiting ambulance. He must have been thankful to arrive at the West Cornwall Hospital. When I visited him later on he was suffering from pneumonia - little wonder, considering the shock and exposure he had suffered in his helpless condition.

With all the flooding and material damage as well as the gale force winds it was amazing that there were so few casualties. One fisherman broke an arm as he jumped from one boat to another in the harbour, and amid all this turmoil, as men struggled to secure their tossing craft, this was the only real injury.

I remember my own good fortune as I made my way along the backs of some houses noting how much water was being dashed against the roofs. One chimney looked in danger of collapsing at any moment and I decided to climb a garden wall and retreat in another direction. Imagine my surprise when I dropped into a large water tank on the other side. Having extricated myself, only just a little wetter than I was before, I decided to take a chance on the chimney. Certain mental pictures still remain. The sight of Mrs. Ball standing at the top of her stairs as we tried to salvage some of her property, repeating over and over again, "'Tis all finished for now, Vicar."

Some things had their humorous side and I remember being fascinated by the sight of a very large lady in her night clothes standing in her downstairs bathroom, bucket

It's Only the Vicar

in hand, and bailing water into her bath. Considering the fact that the level of the sea was everywhere higher than the plug-hole in the bath it amazed me that the water continued to run away!

There were those who worked tirelessly in the rescue work that went on all day, including Jack Kirkwood of the R.N.M.D.S.F. and the ever-faithful and stalwart P.C. Owen Bulford. Various relief organizations were soon on the scene and I was amazed to be greeted just after mid-day by two members of the Church Army who had travelled all the way from London to see where they could give help and relief.

Certain makeshift measures had to be taken before nightfall when the next high tide was due. Many were engaged in filling and carrying sand-bags as the work of salvaging household goods went on. Many people in Newlyn had to evacuate their homes, as did many in the Wherry Town area of Penzance. This was very largely supervised by the police who were anxious to see that nobody was left in a home where there was any danger. Newlyn vicarage was bursting at the seams that night as we accommodated as many as possible of those in need. The family from the Mission were among them, since their windows had all been smashed by the waves and the place was no longer habitable.

The following morning we were greatly relieved to find the wind and the tide subsiding. Some people were very early on the scene, including the Mayor of Penzance, Alderman Matthews, of Gulval. He was just coming across to speak to me when he realised, in his hurry to be on the scene, he had forgotten to put in his false teeth. In the circumstances, as he explained later, he felt that just a friendly wave was more appropriate.

Some time was to elapse before some of the more unfortunate people could return to their homes, many of which would never be quite the same again. But most impressive was the attitude taken by the people of Newlyn at this time. There was no panic, there were no complaints, just a willingness to get on and put things right, with still

A Feel of the Sea

plenty of humour as they compared their plight, one with another. To live in Newlyn at that time was to share the life of the sea, its fortunes and misfortunes, and, above all, to be one with the families of this community who shared such a common interest.

In these circumstances it was a special joy to me to be invited to become an honorary chaplain to the Missions to Seamen, with the special ministry of visiting the men of the lighthouses around the Cornish coast, as well as the crew of the Sevenstones lightship off the Isles of Scilly. For quite some time the Missions to Seamen had a special arrangement, (perhaps relationship would be a better word), with Trinity House, whereby chaplains could visit the men who do this very important and exacting work of safeguarding the lives of those who sail on the high seas. The main role of Trinity House is to warn mariners of the dangerous rocks which surround our coastline and, at the same time, to give them navigational aids to enable them to chart their passage through safe waters. In addition it marks wrecks and provides pilotage wherever it is needed.

When I began this work I did so under the watchful eye of Captain Parnell, a retired captain from the Royal Navy, who organized the work of the various chaplains with meticulous efficiency. Although he was in his eightieth year when I joined this service he was still very active and quite nimble and paid regular visits to each district.

From the moment that I met the crew of *T.H.V. Stella* and her commander, Capt. C.C.C. Parsons O.B.E., I felt completely at home and I am so grateful for all the kindness and courtesy they showed me during those nine very happy years. Indeed, I still value the friendships that I made then among the members of the Service and their families. At that time helicopters had not come on the scene and the lightship reliefs went by sea, rather than by air.

The crew of the *Stella* numbered about thirty-seven men which meant that I had a fair-sized little company to visit during the voyage to and fro, as well as being able to talk to the reliefs on their way out, or to the men returning home for their fortnight ashore.

It's Only the Vicar

Few people will know what happens during the relief of a lighthouse or lightship, so let me recall briefly how things went some twenty-five years ago when I first became associated with this service.

The Sevenstones lightship was invariably relieved on a Tuesday. That meant that the men going out for their term afloat would spend part of Monday making sure their provisions were put aboard the *Stella* to last them for the four weeks they would be away from home. If she left in the early hours of Tuesday morning, then they would spend the night aboard, and quite often I did the same, rather than rise at some unearthly hour. Getting the ship out of Penzance dock was no easy feat; it took a lot of skill, especially if there was a wind to catch the superstructure as she went through the gates.

From Penzance there would be about two-and-a-half to three hours' sailing time to reach the lightship where the crew would be waiting to receive us. The Master of the *Stella* would then bring her towards the stern of the lightvessel as far as conditions would allow, pick up a buoy carrying a line and pull in the hawser which would secure the vessels at a safe distance from one another. Hoses would then be pulled across to supply water and oil to the lightship.

Meanwhile the boat would be plying to and fro, carrying men and supplies. Quite often the main load would be coal and anthracite. There was always something special about hearing the call, "Stand by the boat!" followed soon after by, "Boat's away!" Occasionally, an engineer would also have to make the trip to do some maintenance of essential equipment.

My hope was always to get across with the first boat to enable me to spend as long as possible with the men who were just half-way through their shift. Having paid my respects to the Master, I would then be able to join in the various activities going on as stores were landed and anthracite stowed in the hold. In this way no time was wasted and we could, at the same time, talk on any matters of interest. There were times when one of the crew would have a problem of a very practical nature to discuss. It could well be that he was concerned about something to do with his home, and an offer to see the housing manager when I returned would often put his mind at ease.

I remember a rather special moment during one of these reliefs which happened as I was leaving. Men who had received letters from home naturally chose the earliest possible moment to read them. As I popped my head around a corner to say my farewells to a most likeable crewman, he looked up from his letter and I saw that all was not as it should be.

"Everything all right?" I asked, "I'm afraid not," came the reply. "Anything I can do?" I enquired. He pushed a sheet of paper in front of me and said, "What the hell do you make of that?"

The letter was from his wife to say that she considered their marriage was more or less at an end. There was no time to discuss the matter; the boat was now waiting, but, I promised to see his family doctor to see if he could help, since this news was all out of keeping with the normally happy person we knew his wife to be.

The doctor was a little apprehensive about making an approach in these circumstances and, as he explained, he could not just go charging in without being called. However, one of the sons had just done very well in his examinations, and the doctor decided to pop in and offer his congratulations. He discovered that the lad's mother was far from well and in the midst of an endogenous depression. Happily, by the time her husband returned from sea she was well on the way to making a recovery and all was well.

Such incidents make one aware of how precious time is on such occasions. But no matter how pressing the issue, one must never keep a crew and boat waiting. Always an eye had to be kept on the weather as well as on the light and the state of the tides. Quite often a buoy such as the Runnelstone would have to be checked or serviced, while it sometimes happened that the relief of Round Island (one of the Scilly's group) would be undertaken on the same day.

It's Only the Vicar

Time was even more precious when relieving a lighthouse such as Wolf Rock. Here there is a very limited landing stage which means needing to arrive just before low-water to give the men the opportunity to erect their hoisting tackle, and, hope and pray that conditions would be calm enough for the relief to proceed in safety.

The commander of the Trinity House vessel has a very special responsibility at such times. Naturally he would like to be able to relieve on time so that the men could get home to their families, but he must not endanger lives during the operation.

I have seen a commander spending a long time on the bridge staring through his binoculars to see how clear the landing stage might be and for how long. He would have an eye for that extra high wave which builds up every four or five minutes. They had a saying to which they kept very religiously, "When in doubt, don't."

The very first lighthouse that I visited was the Longships just off Lands End. On that day there was a strong easterly wind blowing, which meant that, as we handled the coal and anthracite and hoisted it into the lighthouse we became more and more grimy with the effect of the fine dust and the spray from the sea. The relief, because of these conditions, took rather longer than anticipated so that, by the time we returned to the *Stella*, darkness had come down like a blanket.

By the time the men on the Longships had got to the lantern-house to operate the great light, we were just getting under way and I shall never forget seeing that first great shaft of light as it pierced through the darkness. It brought with it a new meaning to some words in the first chapter of St. John's Gospel, "The light shineth in darkness, and the darkness comprehended it not ..." With the coming of Christ into this world the darkness had been cleft as with some great beam of light, a light that would go on shining down the generations, and nothing would be able to encroach upon it.

Arriving back at Penzance we found a luxury yacht tied up at the steps where we were to make our landing. The

A Feel of the Sea

owner viewed us with obvious displeasure as we moored alongside this spotless craft and took the only possible course of clambering across her decks with all our baggage.

That same evening there was a reception in St. John's Hall and, as the Mayor's chaplain, I was expected to be present. After a lot of scrubbing, I duly presented myself and joined one of the groups of people who stood around engaged in small talk as is customary at these functions. I could not help hearing part of a conversation going on near me, and I pricked up my ears when I heard someone say, "Yes, and they had the audacity to climb right across my boat; they were filthy and looked like a lot of bloody blacks."

Soon after this the Mayor himself joined the group and beckoned me across to meet them. "I would like you to meet my chaplain," he said to the owner of the luxury yacht. As we shook hands I had to say, "I believe we have, in fact, already met."

"I don't recall it, then," came the reply. "Oh yes," I said, "Not many hours ago. In fact I was one of the bloody blacks!"

People often ask what kind of services we held when I visited the lighthouse men. Some enquirers appear a little surprised, if not actually shocked, when I say, "Well in fact, we don't hold sevices except on special occasions." There are of course other ways of ministering to people in our Lord's Name and I always set a special value on the times when we talked about our religious beliefs and aspirations. In fact there was never any problem about raising such fundamental issues with men, who, by their nature and the nature of their calling, were deeply religious.

Certain very special moments stand out in my memory. I have still in my mind a picture of all the men on the Sevenstones Lightship standing along the rail in rather blustery conditions, just two days before Christmas, and singing "O come, all ye faithful ...", followed by the Christmas Collect, the Prayer For Those At Sea, and the Lord's Prayer.

Then one Christmas Eve, just as I was about to set off

It's Only the Vicar

for the Midnight Eucharist, the phone bell rang. It was Land's End Radio to say that they had the crew of the Sevenstones on the air and they wished to send their best wishes to me and my family for a very Happy Christmas. It made me feel very happy indeed, but at the same time very humble, that these men who were away from home on a little craft tossing on the Atlantic Roll should think about me. It certainly helped to keep life in some kind of perspective.

We need a reminder like that from time to time for it is all too easy to go through life without a thought for those who spend so much time at sea ensuring the safety of mariners and fishermen. It is hard to imagine the conditions on the Sevenstones during some of the winter months when high winds mean huge waves for weeks on end. How do you cook anything on a cooker which changes its angle so drastically every few seconds? Our fishermen are aware of the great benefits of the lights which guide them safely on their way, and quite often show their appreciation. They will often go out of their way to throw a few freshly caught fish to the crew aboard the lightship and also volunteer to take any messages to people at home. Yet, as far as the general public are concerned, the men who man our lighthouses and lightships are almost a forgotten race.

Many years ago, before the advent of television, when we relied upon our radios, there used to be a Christmas broadcast which linked the Commonwealth together before the Sovereign gave us his Christmas message. Quite often this included the voice of one of our lighthouse keepers as a reminder of those who had to spend Christmas away from home. I seem to remember that Edward Ward, one of the B.B.C. commentators at that time, spent Christmas on a lighthouse because he had missed the boat.

The Royal Navy notwithstanding, Trinity House is THE Senior Service, having been granted its charter by Henry VIII in 1514. At that time it was laid down that the guild of Master Mariners, now brought into being formally, be known as "The Master, Wardens and Assistants of the

A Feel of the Sea

Guild, Fraternity or Brotherhood of the Most Glorious and Undivided Trinity and of St. Clement in the Parish of Deptford Strond in the County of Kent." I find the title more glorious than understandable and there has always been some doubt about who St. Clement might have been. The St. Clement who was one of the first Bishops of Rome in about 100 A.D. must have been intended as he has been regarded as the patron saint of mariners. There was some kind of corporation in existence before 1514, but records have been lost. On several occasions fire has destroyed Trinity House's valuable records and priceless relics, notably in the Great Fire of 1666 and again in 1714, while in 1940, the headquarters was damaged by fire during the air raids.

Among its relics is a small item, of no particular value in itself, an oval-shaped piece of lead weighing 7 ozs., which is of considerable interest to those who live in the West Country and know something of the history of the Eddystone Lighthouse. After the ill-fated Winstanley tower had been completely demolished in a terrible storm on the night of November 26th 1703, causing the death of the Winstanley and all those who were with him, the task of erecting a replacement was given to an amateur architect, John Rudyerd.

Rudyerd designed his tower on quite different lines from that of Winstanley. It was slim by comparison enabling it to withstand the gales which rage in those parts. However it was susceptible to fire and this tragedy struck on the night of December 1st 1755. For the three keepers it was a terrible ordeal as they tried to shelter throughout the night from the inferno above them with all the dangers from falling timbers, redhot bolts and molten lead. Henry Hall, the eldest of the three - and they were all well on in years - was nearly ninety years old. He complained to his companions that he had swallowed some molten lead as he looked up with mouth agape. They had little time nor concern for this at the time but, after they were rescued and taken to hospital, poor Henry still complained of the pain in his stomach. He was thought to be delirious when he told them the cause. Although after a few days he sat up in bed and ate some solid food he died just a week later. A post-mortem examination showed his story to be true; he had swallowed the lead, all seven ounces of it.

Much of the splended tradition associated with Trinity House still remains, although much of the splendour associated with Trinity Monday has been lost. There was a time when the elected Master and Wardens made a great procession to Deptford Green in London and processed to St. Nicholas, the Mother Church of the Navy. Before the service the vicar administered the sacred oath of allegiance. After the service there was a great banquet in Trinity House. At Newlyn we used to mark the religious background of Trinity House with a special service on Trinity Sunday when serving members took part in Evensong, the men in uniform.

The governing body still remains in the hands of the Elder Brethren. Not only are they, almost without exception, fine seamen with a proud record of service but they maintain that tradition of courtesy long associated with naval officers, together with a deep religious feeling. On those few occasions when I have approached them about the men and their problems I have been listened to with real concern and, wherever they have been able to help, they have readily done so.

Each year the Elder Brethren made their inspection of each District aboard the *Patricia*. This event was always anticipated by an inspection carried out by the Superintendent of the District, so that all should go well on the great day itself.

The first time I was invited aboard to meet these distinguished men of the sea was to join them for pre-luncheon drinks. I arrived soon after noon, having taken three services but not having had breakfast. It was a glorious summer's day and I was not slow to take what looked like a glass of orangeade from a tray carried by one of the stewards.

In keeping with typical naval hospitality my glass was never allowed to get very low before being topped up

A Feel of the Sea

again. It was a happy gathering and time passed quickly as I met old friends and was introduced to people I had not met previously. When the time came for me to leave I was conscious of walking down the gangway on air, and there waiting patiently on the quayside was my little blue Wolseley. She must have thought me rather ungracious when I took one look at her and decided to walk home.

At that time Trinity House represented a great family with a common interest, and there was a wonderful feeling of caring and fellowship among all these men regardless of rank. Certain things must change but I hope that that spirit still prevails. That spirit was exemplified in a little incident which happened at sea, just before Christmas, in a year when we were having particularly bad weather. The Wolf Rock was overdue for relief and the *Stella* had been standing by in the late evening, waiting for low-tide, in the hope that a landing might be possible. The time came and passed and the landing stage was still awash, darkness was approaching and the wind was still freshening. Reluctantly the ship's commander turned away and decided that, rather than return to Mount's Bay with nothing accomplished, we should make towards the Sevenstones light-vessel. We arrived to undertake what turned out to be a very lumpy relief.

The little lightship was certainly tossing as we got aboard and wrestled with bags of anthracite and coal and manhandled drums and provisions aboard. By the time that we had got away to return to the *Stella,* the wind had strengthened so much that we were told to keep our distance as the commander of the ship attempted to give us some lee-water, in the hope that he could pick us up without fear of damaging the boat.

We had a most experienced and first-rate coxswain at the helm of our little craft. Jimmy Quick was a Mousehole man who had spent his younger days as a fisherman. As he manoeuvred into the most favourable position I wondered in my mind what course he would take if we could not be picked up. Would he make for the shelter of The Scillies perhaps, or make the long trip back to

It's Only the Vicar

Penzance in an open boat? I recall Jimmy with his boots unlaced and hand on the rudder, quite unperturbed as he turned to me and said, "I don't think there were quite as many in church at Paul Feast this year." I have to confess that, at that particular moment, I was not terribly concerned about the statistics of Paul Feast. Certainly it seemed the coxswain's mind was on higher things but, at the same time I have a feeling that this was a bit of the most profound applied psychology, although it is doubtful Jimmy would have admitted to that.

Morwenna

If variety is the spice of life, then my next appointment as a chaplain was bound to bring a little spice, since the work involved was completely different from the previous one. Almost from the time I went to Newlyn I was a member of the committee of Social and Moral Welfare and had a very special interest in the work of Morwenna. This was the house in Lescudjack Terrace, Penzance, which cared for unmarried mothers as well as being a place of refuge for any girl finding herself in difficulties.

Although I am in no way a committee man, and still find meetings something to be endured, I did enjoy the meetings held at Morwenna. This was in no small measure because the meetings were presided over by Mrs. Charles Williams, of Trewidden, who was an excellent chairman with plenty of vision and a practical approach to every situation. She had a delightful sense of humour which she used very effectively whenever we took ourselves too seriously or were in danger of becoming too emotionally involved in any particular case.

When I was asked if I would act as chaplain to the home as well as being a committee member, I welcomed the opportunity of becoming more closely involved with the good work being done there.

At that time we were fortunate in having for the matron Mrs. Gibbons, who came from St. Mary's on the Isles of Scilly. Her husband, like many Islanders, had been associated with boats, but he died suddenly, leaving his widow to care for their daughters. It was a real blessing for the home when she came across to the mainland to take up her appointment at Morwenna, for she was not only well-trained for these duties, but she was herself an understanding mother with daughters of her own, and a warm and homely personality.

In addition to Mrs. Gibbons we had a delightful and radiantly happy assistant in the person of Miss Lee. No matter what the mood in the home, and no matter what the problem might be, never once did Miss Lee lose her sense of composure or fail to see some good side to whatever was going on. I went to see these good ladies to find out what was expected of me and how best I could fit into the general running of the home.

It was agreed that it would be most helpful if I dropped in informally as often as possible to give the girls the opportunity to know me well enough to be able to speak freely about anything they wished to discuss, either as a group, or in private. There would of course be the times when I would come in for a general talk or to show slides on some topic of interest.

At the conclusion of our little discussion, Matron turned to me and said, "I need hardly remind you not to make the same mistake as your predecessor when he was first appointed." He was a very saintly person and getting well on in years, and I was all ears to know just where he could have put a foot wrong. Evidently he had talked at some length to the girls on moral issues and had concluded by saying, "Now, in the future, if ever you feel tempted, remember you can always send for me."

Running a home for unmarried mothers, as well as for those who find themselves in dire circumstances, means that the atmosphere created is all-important. It takes only one of the company to feel resentful and determined not to fit in with the rest to upset the running of the whole "family". Fortunately, most of the girls were only too thankful to find themselves in a caring and understanding home, and responded in a helpful manner. Nearly always you could count on having one of the residents who turned out to be something of a comedian, which helped to reduce any tension when they had to be in one room together for any length of time.

Various little happenings soon showed that I was being accepted as a member of this family. One girl, Dai, who had originated from Wales, was expecting her baby about two or three weeks after she arrived. Matron, or one of the staff, usually let me know when any of the girls went into the Bolitho Maternity Home, which was quite near the Vicarage, so that I could visit them there. I was, therefore, a little surprised when I went to Morwenna one afternoon and found that Dai was not there and was told that she had gone into hospital.

"And why wasn't I told?" I asked. "Well, you see there were problems, and it meant that she had to go to Redruth, but everything is all right now and she has actually got her boy." "So she had set her heart on a boy," I remarked in all innocence. "Oh yes, she very much wanted a boy so that she could call it Harold after you." I duly expressed my appreciation of the honour, with the suggestion that it might be prudent for this not to happen very often.

At least Dai was free to choose without much interference or adverse comment from her family, unlike another mother from Newlyn at about that time. All had gone well with the confinement and a great-aunt who called at the home to enquire was happy to find that a lovely little girl had been born. "What are they going to call her then?" the old lady enquired. "Hazel," came the reply. There was a brief pause while great-aunt reflected, then, in her delightful Irish accent she made her pronouncement. "Three-hundred-and-sixty-five days in a year and a blessed saint for each one of them, and they've got to call her after a nut."

The girls who found their way into Morwenna often came from broken homes and, in the main, had not had a happy time at school. There were exceptions and those with an academic background were sometimes thought of as snobs - at times with a little justification. Yet one could

It's Only the Vicar

appreciate the fact that a girl who wished to continue her studies could find pop music and endless chatter rather distracting. My experience with them led me to the conclusion that they rather enjoyed the simple things of life and would be quite happy with slide-shows on various topics. At that time I had a film-strip on the life and travels of St. Paul and this turned out to be a favourite with nearly all the girls. During one of these sessions an apologetic Miss Lee (she was a devout Roman Catholic), came into the room and asked if I could break off for a short while and be of assistance in another direction.

It was not at all unusual for me to have to bring the car around to the gate to act as an ambulance to transport an expectant mother to the maternity home. This was exactly what I was expecting to do on this occasion but found that I was mistaken. As soon as we were alone, Miss Lee explained in a few hurried sentences that their little dog had escaped through the door when one of the girls entered, adding with some concern, that this was hardly the time for her to be running wild in Penzance.

"Do you think you could help me to get her back, Father?" she asked with great earnestness, adding, "I feel a bit responsible with Mrs. Gibbons away, and she left such strict instructions about being sure to keep her in."

It was quite late and dark as we set out in the direction of the recreation field. I had by far outstripped Miss Lee by the time I discovered our quarry. It was not difficult to assess the situation; it appeared more like the meet of the local foxhounds, with every dog in the area seemingly in attendance. I met our dear assistant matron as she came up the rise, very much out of breath, and explained that, while I had found her it was rather too late in the day.

"Never mind Father," came the reply from the ever-cheerful Miss Lee, "at least you've done your best and she's had the blessing of the Church, which is more than can be said for a lot of them."

Some weeks later I was working in the study and the incident was almost forgotten, when the phone bell rang. It was Mrs. Gibbons with an enquiry. "Could you tell me the date of St. Paul's missionary journeys?" I must confess that the question gave me quite a lot of satisfaction. So the girls really had been taking some of this in and discussing it among themselves I thought. After a moment or two to reflect I said, "Well, possibly about 46 A.D." "In that case our little bitch is long overdue," came the quick reply.

At that moment the penny dropped and I realised the date in question was that on which I had shown the slides and our little canine friend had made her escape. After consulting my diary we got it right, and Matron was able to work out just when that particular confinement should take place.

I am always intrigued by the 'question and answer' pages that appear in certain magazines, especially those dealing with personal problems. From my own experience with the girls at Morwenna as well as in parish life generally, I have found that it usually takes hours of patient listening, a lot of understanding, encouragement and support to be of any real help. However, I expect there are those who just need an answer to a particular question which can be found in the pages of their favourite publication.

One question that arose frequently and inevitably in the home concerned the future of the child who was expected. Is the mother going to be able to keep it, or will it be adopted almost at once? Thankfully there were certain procedures to be followed very carefully, and besides this we had a team of ladies, not only well-trained in all aspects of adoption, including the legal implications, but also blessed with empathy and intuition which makes all the difference.

Often a girl who was quite adamant about what would happen to her baby, changed completely after the child had been born and she had held and fed her baby. Quite often one could sense that there was 'something going on' when an adoption was taking place. In nearly all cases, everything went smoothly but I have known cases which have caused some distress either to the mother or to the adopting parents.

It's Only the Vicar

In one particular instance where I had been asked to act as a referee, there was a very happy sequel to the story. The husband and wife, who longed to have a baby, had experienced some difficulty in following the necessary procedures since he worked with the meteorological department in the R.A.F. and was constantly on the move. However, with the understanding on the part of those concerned, an adoption of a little girl by the name of Rachel was arranged. On the day that the court should have been sitting to make the final ruling, there was much snow and ice on the roads, resulting in the court being postponed for a fortnight. During those two weeks the natural mother reappeared on the scene and decided to have her baby back. After having the child in their home, the would-be adoptive parents were terribly upset and, to make things appear even worse, it was just before Christmas.

At that time there happened to be a quite hefty baby by the name of Malcolm in need of fostering so, to relieve the situation the young couple were asked to have him over the Christmas period. They readily agreed to this and quite took to the child although he was so different from the dainty little girl they had given up. When Malcolm came up for adoption it was quite natural that the couple who were fostering him should be given the first opportunity, which they were pleased to respond to, and all went well in this case for them.

However, while all this was going on, Rachel's mother abandoned her baby, leaving her on the door-step of a farm house. In the circumstances it was felt only right to ask this young couple who had been so disappointed at giving her up, if they would like to have Rachel and start all over again. They were only too happy to do this and so found that they had a lovely family, a boy and a girl, with only a month or so difference in their ages. It was a very happy moment for me, as well as for them, when we all gathered around the font for the christening of these two children so fortunate to find such a loving and caring home.

It is a great joy to me to be in touch with some of these children who have been adopted and to follow their progress. Some are now married themselves and have children of their own. How good it is to see some of the loving care which has been bestowed on them by people like Mrs. Gibbons and Miss Lee, and their adoptive parents who have given them secure and happy homes, reflected in another generation.

Of recent years my work as a hospital chaplain has brought me into close touch with those who have sought a way out of their problems through abortion. When this is actually happening is hardly the time for moralising, but I have never failed to give a firm answer if a patient has asked directly how I felt about abortion. In the whole of my experience there is no joy or happiness to be found when this course is followed, and often one finds there are those who go through a period of depression and mental anguish, even though they say they have no religious scruples to trouble them.

Besides this I have seen the distress abortion has caused to so many of the nursing staff who have found themselves with divided loyalties. I remember one nursing sister who experienced a complete breakdown, largely because of the stress she was under, and had to give up her work. Morwenna may have brought with it some problems and some heartaches but there was much joy and happiness. And certainly there are some wonderful young men and women growing to maturity themselves, as well as their mums, who can be truly thankful, to say nothing of the immense gratitude felt by all those couples who have adopted children from that particular home. I certainly look back and give thanks for the privilege of being associated with Morwenna, its committee, its staff and, above all, the girls I have known and their offspring.

Letter from America

Ever since I was at St. Mawgan I had kept in touch with a certain John May, his wife, Gwen, and their children, Gwennie and Tre. The friendship began when John came home from the United States to visit his aged grandmother who, at that time, lived in a little bungalow called Hylton overlooking the village of St. Mawgan. She was a charming old lady and I used to visit her regularly until the time of her death.

It was always a great joy when John and his family were to be seen in church. They were readily recognizable as coming from America by the 'cute' style of their dress. I was glad to find that they were all very much involved in church life where they lived in Washington. John was, in fact, a Reader in the Episcopal Church and he was delighted when I asked him to take part in the services at the old parish church where he had been brought up, and which still held such a place in his affection. It did, however, come as a complete surprise to me when I received a letter from America inviting me to come over and take care of Holy Cross Mission for a short time. In his letter John had briefly outlined the circumstances which prompted this unexpected invitation.

The year was 1967 and the war in Vietnam was still dragging on. The U.S. Under Secretary for Defence had asked Canon Dick Williams, then Rector of Holy Cross, to visit the American Chaplaincies in the conflict area to encourage them in their work and to bring back a report.

Letter from America

When Canon Williams returned he was a sick man having picked up nearly every bug in the Far East and, perhaps more than this, he was sick at heart at what he had found during his tour. His church council had met and decided he should have a complete rest, and it was then that John May had suggested that he had me over for a short while to fill the gap.

As it happened, it was about this time that some welcome help had come to Newlyn. David Carpenter, whose home was in Somerset, was about to be ordained and looking for a place to serve his Title. I met him when he came to look at some of the churches in the Penzance area, among them St. Peter's Newlyn. Since we were looking for an assistant curate at Newlyn, we approached the Bishop who agreed that he should come and assist in the parish as soon as he had been ordained to the Sacred Ministry. He had now been long enough in the parish to know the general working of the place, and the people, and it was a good thing for him to have me out of the way for a short while so that he could feel his feet.

When it became known in Newlyn that I was off to America for a month, there were all kinds of reaction. Not long before I was due to leave I was doing my annual "penance" sitting on Newlyn Bridge to collect some money for our two churches. I can still picture Harold Jewell, from the fish and chip shop opposite where I was seated, coming across to make the first contribution of the day.

Before putting the £5 note he held in his hand into the box he paused. "You're off to America, I hear," he said. When I affirmed that this was indeed the case, he simply put the note back in his pocket with the remark, "In that case you can pay for your own holiday." This was the delightful sense of humour we shared in Newlyn, and I am quite sure that the £5 note found its way into the box before the day was out.

There were a number of requests from various people for me to contact relatives in the U.S. One dear old lady, who lived on the Gwavas Estate, asked if I would visit her sister while I was over there. When I asked for her address she told me that this was the real problem and the very reason why she wanted me to look her up. They had been out of touch for some years and the last they had heard of her was that she had moved to the Pittsburgh area. She thought that, "since you were over there, you could make some enquiries and then make a call."

The best I could do was to say that, should I find myself in Pittsburgh I would keep an eye out for her! In the event I did manage to get in touch with a few relatives, whose names had been given to me, by telephone.

Words fail me to describe the warmth of the reception I received from the moment I arrived in Washington. The May family could not possibly have been more kind and they did everything for my comfort and entertainment. The night after my arrival they gave a very special kind of party, and I well remember that frogs' legs and blueberry pie were on the menu.

That evening I learned a lot about the American way of life, including the fact that you do not make casual remarks about things which you never expect to happen. Among the guests was a prominent cancer surgeon and I expressed my interest in the way that hospitals were run in the States as compared with the way we did things back home.

"Right," said the surgeon, "as soon as the party is over let's get back to the hospital and I'll introduce you to some of the staff and you can spend the whole night there if you feel like it." This was the way they approached life: you get on with it there and then.

Another offer I received that evening came from The Revd. Fred Arterton, who was then Principal of the College of Preachers at Washington Cathedral. This was to spend a day with him to see the great Cathedral of St. Peter and St. Paul which was still under construction. This was indeed a day to remember. The cathedral stands on the highest elevation in that area, and is a truly magnificent sight. Built in Gothic style, it stands as a symbol of the faith of the American people and a reminder that building a cathedral after the same pattern and in the same tradition of former centuries is still a possibility. (When Pierre L'Enfant had

Letter from America

designed the City of Washington with such extraordinary vision, he had spoken of a great national church as part of his scheme, and in 1850 a Sunday school teacher had left forty gold coins which secured this unique site on which building was begun in the year 1907.)

What struck me in the course of that memorable day was the way that this work was being carried out at the end of the 20th century. Although so many men were at work, there was no noise or commotion of any kind. Craftsmen had been gathered from all parts of the world and many of these little groups who worked together came from the same family. I watched, as some of them worked quietly on delicate carving beneath the vaulted roof, while others worked outside on the main structure. One recent happening of particular interest to me was the arrival of a peal of bells made in Loughborough and their hanging was almost complete. I was privileged to be able to ascend the tower in a lift, which had just come into use, rather than toil up the hard way.

My first Sunday at Holy Cross was rather special. The services themselves were hardly any different from those I had left in Newlyn and I could adapt myself readily to those little variations such as praying for the President instead of Her Majesty the Queen.

What particularly delighted me was the way people made the effort to be in that particular place on this Sunday because of their Cornish connections. The day before, the Washington Post had carried an announcement that a Cornish priest who visited lighthouses around that part of the United Kingdom would be conducting the services and preaching at Holy Cross. This piece of information had brought some representatives from the U.S. Lighthouse Service. Among those present because of their Cornish ancestry was the daughter of Police Superintendent Sidney Keast, of Truro, with her family and, even closer to Newlyn, the grand-daughter of dear old Mrs. Hoare of Kenstella Road at Newlyn, someone I knew very well. Gwen May quickly invited some of these people back to her home so that we could get to know them better.

It's Only the Vicar

Mrs. Hoare's descendant, Sheila Firesteine, had been in the world of entertainment as a dancer, and she and her husband became regular visitors during my stay. On one of these visits Sheila had asked me if I would mind taking back a little package for her Gran when I returned to Newlyn and I readily consented. Had I known the contents I would not have felt so comfortable as I passed through customs. In fact it was a year or more later that I learned that I had been the means of getting some of the family jewellery back where it belonged! "They would hardly search a clergyman" was the reason for choosing me for this particular job.

The people I met whilst I was in the U.S. were all interested in life in Cornwall and, in particular, my work among the fisherfolk of Newlyn. For my part I was finding the great city of Washington full of interest each day that I was there. One blessing, as far as I was concerned, was the orderly way the city is laid out from the Capitol at the heart of the city. From this centre the well-known avenues of Independence and Constitution and all the others spread out like spokes from some great cartwheel. Intersecting them at regular intervals and in circles are the main streets designated by the letters of the alphabet. Washington is particularly beautiful at night with its very special illuminations for all the many elaborate memorials such as the Jefferson Memorial and the National Monument. Reflected light adds to the general effect, much use being made of natural mirrors, stretches of water in well-planned lakes fed from the waters of the Potomac River.

One often hears much about the generosity and the hospitality of the American people, but it is only when you experience all this that you realize the lengths they will go to, just to make sure that everything is being done for your happiness. When I went to watch a baseball match being played by their top teams in the huge stadium, I was afforded the best possible seat and given the opportunity to meet many of the leading figures. They presented me with a ball inscribed by all the Washington Senators as well as one of their special caps.

Letter from America

Early one morning I was taken to the White House with a special pass so that I could see over this renowned building before President Nixon needed it for his own particular use! The rooms were certainly very beautiful but what struck me most was that, later that day, these rooms would all be put to good use. There was a special excitement among the staff on that particular morning since Princess Anne was due to arrive later that day to attend a ball.

My hosts made sure that I saw something of the countryside as well as the City of Washington itself. I was taken for a drive through Virginia and Maryland and saw something of the vastness and the beauty of these parts. As we went down to Chesapeake Bay we were stopped by a police patrol car because John was exceeding the speed limit. John immediately got out of the car and walked towards the policeman to ask what the problem was. (He explained to me later that it was wise to do this in the United States to show that you are not going to pull out a gun or do something of this nature.) On hearing what was wrong John, with great composure, remarked that he was glad in a way, since his passenger happened to be a priest from the Old Country and he could now actually see the American police in action. "Well, in that case," replied the officer, "say we just treat this as a caution." Afterwards my friend explained that he had been in a slight dilemma since he could not be sure whether this good officer was a Catholic or a Protestant but he had hopefully phrased his comment so that he could cover either persuasion!

On my last Sunday at Holy Cross, one of the churchwardens, a certain Bob Buehler, a man of tremendous drive and energy, asked me if I had seen all that I wanted to during my stay. Jokingly I remarked that I had been here for these weeks without visiting the Capitol itself to see how this great country was governed. Bob pounced on this immediately and, within a matter of hours after I had arrived back with the May family, the phone was ringing and the whole thing had been arranged for me to spend a day at the Capitol as the guest of Congressman Mize.

It's Only the Vicar

When the day came, everything was carefully planned for me from the time I arrived at the steps of that great building. I was taken to the office of Congressman Mize and delighted to find that he was the nephew of a well-known bishop in West Africa. Since I had said something to Bob Buehler about wanting to know "how the thing worked," I was given a tour of the various parts of the Capitol to show how an idea conceived in the mind of a member went through various stages and committees until as law it was finally sanctioned. Lunch with some of the Congressmen was a very jovial affair before I was taken to hear the Senate debating Vietnam, and I became aware of what was meant by 'The Hawks' and 'The Doves'.

The moment that remains most embedded in my mind as I think back to this day was the short time I spent in the Prayer Room at the heart of the Capitol. There I had been able to say my prayers before the altar with the stained glass window above it depicting George Washington at prayer.

When the time arrived for my departure I was already beginning to think of home and all that awaited me there, and I certainly left the U.S. with many happy memories, and just a little wiser than when I had arrived. This was, perhaps, particularly so in the case of the Vietnam war. Here in the U.K. we followed what was happening with a certain indifference. However, to be there among people who came to you to share their anxiety about a son who was just leaving for that area of bitter conflict, or to have a relative come to you in great sorrow because they had just received news that one of the family had been killed, brought home the stark reality that war is war, wherever it may be.

It was such a joy to be able to return to my family and hear all the news of the people of Newlyn. "The Cornishman" carried an account of my impressions of the people of Washington, and a number of invitations came my way to speak to various organizations. Fortunately I had come home with a quantity of colour slides which made this task much easier than it could have been. During the months that followed my visit I was also to receive a

Letter from America

number of books connected with the Capitol, including all the inaugural speeches made by each President from George Washington to the present time. It was good to know that my hosts had not forgotten me. I had certainly not forgotten them.

Home Again

There is a saying that 'No man hath seen England who hath only England seen.' Certainly there is an underlying truth in this statement which can be appreciated only after being away from the homeland for a length of time. Inevitably, there is the tendency to make comparisons between what you have experienced abroad and what you come home to again. This is true of the climate, the landscape and, more especially, the way that people live.

The pace of life in the capital city of the U.S.A. is lively, to say the least. People appeared to work very hard and they enjoyed their social life to the full, filling every moment with some kind of activity. Something else which impressed me was the abundance of everything needed for daily living. In the giant super-stores there were masses of meat together with all kinds of food which I had not seen in such abundance before. The size and the variety of fruit and vegetables alone was staggering.

It was therefore with a certain amount of relief that I returned to share the much simpler life-style of the people of Newlyn and to be able once more to share their joys and sorrows, their hopes and fears.

This chapter will be taken up with reflections on some of the family occasions which go to make up the life and particular character of any community. To pretend that Newlyn had no problems and no falling short of the accepted moral code would be to blind one's eyes to the facts. What was, however, true about this little community

Home Again

was the fact that there was no pretence and no hypocrisy about the way they lived. Sin and evil were recognized for what they are, and there was never any attempt to disguise, or even glamorise unacceptable conduct.

Today, things have changed. Homosexuality is almost generally accepted and we have our gay societies, while on the TV screen it is made to appear as something slightly humorous and little more. A quarter of a century ago in Newlyn this was far from being the case and when I was approached by a young man, seeking help because he had become involved in this practice, it was a matter of very serious consequence, more especially because some youngsters were also involved. It is one thing to speak of these things in vague generalizations and quite another when you are faced with a specific case. Here I was, with a plea for help from a person whose life was apparently in ruins, and having to face up to some serious charges.

Our first meeting took place in St. Peter's Church and this very troubled man was completely frank about his own failings. Never once, during the whole time that I was to be involved in this unhappy affair did I find him anything but honest. Nor did he seek to incriminate anyone else - though he might well have done so.

He must have found very little comfort from that first encounter. Up until that time, I had taken the view that homosexuality was plain wickedness and what was needed was some form of punishment followed up by some very strict discipline to put the matter right. Over the next year or two I was to see a very different side to this tragic and complicated condition.

Two things did impress me at the first meeting. The first I have already mentioned, that there was a ring of truth about all that he told me so candidly. Secondly, he was much concerned for his ageing mother and the distress that the pending court case would inevitably bring to her. I started to visit this frail old lady, and soon discovered that here was at least one of the reasons why her son had departed from the accepted way of life. She had brought up her son all on her own with great care and at no little sacrifice, and in consequence he was devoted to his mother. In fact I suppose it would be true to say that he had closely identified himself with her. Following on from this, when it came to falling in love, he fell in love with the opposite sex from his mother rather than his own.

During the meetings which followed I promised this unfortunate young man that, when the trial took place, I would undertake to let his mother know the outcome. Inevitably, as things were at that time, this meant a prison term of years rather than months, or possibly a suspended sentence. Although I had done my best to prepare his mother for this kind of news, the shock, when it was conveyed to her that the sentence was imprisonment, was quite devastating. One could see the anguish that she was enduring day by day. It was not until the first letters began to arrive from her son that there was a gradual change and she was able to look forward to the time when she would be reunited with him.

While he was serving his sentence I was to learn a lot more about the background to this whole affair. Soon after leaving school he had been taken away from home by two men, each of them having titles and positions of responsibility, to act as a kind of manservant in an all-male establishment. Although I was never offered any evidence, I felt sure in my own mind that it was during this time that he acquired the kind of life-style that was to prove his downfall. At this time I began receiving letters from these two men expressing their concern and, at the same time, offering the kind of financial help that would set him up in a little business on his release. Naturally this tended to confirm the impression I had already formed in my mind.

Although for this particular inmate of H.M. Prison, the time must have seemed endless, for me it seemed an incredibly short time before we were speaking of his return. His mother was full of hope and looked forward to seeing her son respectably set up in his own little business. However, as the time drew nearer for his release there was some obvious stalling from the two would-be benefactors. This I found wholly unacceptable and, since I had kept all

Home Again

their correspondence I felt in quite a strong position to press them for an early fulfilment rather than allow them to disappoint two people who had come to pin their hope for the future upon their promises. I am glad to be able to say that, although the outcome did not fulfil our earliest expectations, enough money was finally forthcoming to enable this man who had served his sentence to set himself up in business in a very modest way.

To say that this was a happy ending to the whole episode would be far from the fact. For a while all went well, but two problems soon emerged. In the first place this man started giving some assistance behind the bar at a local hotel, and this led to his often taking too much to drink. On one such occasion I received a call from the proprietress of the establishment asking me if I could come and give some assistance since he was very drunk and causing a disturbance. This was early one afternoon in the height of the summer season.

After a little difficulty I persuaded him that it was best to make for home and I soon found myself helping a staggering drunk down Market Jew Street. If you have ever tried helping a man in this condition through a crowded street you will have realised that it is fraught with problems, let alone embarrassment. For one thing it is not easy for the casual observer readily to recognize which is the worse for drink or, indeed, onlookers might be forgiven for concluding that both are inebriated. Having become frustrated long enough by his behaviour in a busy street, I decided to go off to the right down the rather steep and narrow road leading towards the harbour area. When my unwelcome companion made another of his staggering lunges in my direction I stepped back and gave him plenty of room to fall. This had a wonderfully sobering effect and we were able to proceed at a much more acceptable pace.

The recourse to the bottle was an indication of some deeper problem and this was soon to come to light. The good-looking young man who had come into his life had decided to return to London, and this proved to be the last straw. One afternoon 'W' appeared at Newlyn vicarage after a violent row with his friend had taken place on the bridge outside the church. Since I was not at home my wife had to deal with the situation. This she did to good effect by taking him into St. Peter's Church and ordering him to get down on his knees and to stay there until I had arrived. Doreen then contacted me at the hospital and I returned as quickly as possible to do my best to restore some level of reasonable understanding.

Evidently my efforts had only a very temporary effect, and this little episode was to be continued rather late that night. About midnight I had a telephone call from Penzance police station requesting me to go immediately to Newlyn Pier to try to persuade a man to give up the idea of throwing himself into the sea. It did not take three guesses as to whom this might be! The weather was appalling, and 'W' appeared as a tragic figure as he stood perched at the edge of the pier. When all the spectators had withdrawn it took only about ten minutes' conversation for him to come to the conclusion that a warm bed might be preferable to a watery grave, and he was soon on his way to the home of a local fisherman nearby who happened to be kindly disposed towards this poor man's plight.

We soon came to the conclusion that the best thing to happen would be to put this drenched (in every sense of the word) individual to bed. Terry was a man of immense physical strength and it was no problem for him to sling this now helpless person over his shoulder and carry him up the stairs. I still recollect seeing a mirror and at least two pictures come down in the process, and the place began to look something of a shambles. Terry's wife appeared on the scene and asked whether she should start clearing up or make a cup of tea. In the circumstances my vote went for a cup of tea.

This was one of the last episodes that I was to be concerned with in as far as this particular saga is concerned. Some years later however, after I had left the parish I received a phone call from this broken-hearted man when his mother died. He had cared for her to the end with great tenderness.

Home Again

Looking back over the years, it is sometimes difficult to know what in your ministry could be termed successful and what, on the other hand was apparent failure. Some ministrations had, to all outward appearances, a happy ending, such as, for example, when after years of effort, a married couple and their three children were at last united in harmony after passing through a time of great stress.

On the other hand one could cite instances where little seemed to be achieved, even after much involvement. This was so often the case where some mental disorder had to be reckoned with. On one occasion, a lady doctor, who was the very essence of compassion and concern, spent some time with me trying to help a particular lady accept a legacy which was due to her. In spite of every assurance we could offer, she refused to accept it or to sign any papers connected with it. She had at one time been in a mental hospital and I suppose that any formalities such as we were trying to follow made her suspicious, and at times quite violent. Since her mother who looked after her could well do with this extra help, a legal answer had eventually to be found to overcome the problem.

Another instance which called for medical assistance concerned a rather mysterious tug which had to be towed into Penzance Harbour. A member of the Press, who happened to know that I was an honorary chaplain to the Missions to Seamen, telephoned me at about 9 p.m. on a winter's night and asked if I knew anything about this craft and conditions aboard, at the same time suggesting that a visit might be well worth while.

It was nearly 10 p.m. by the time I found her tied alongside in complete darkness. Groping my way on board I made out a glimmer of light somewhere beneath the bows. At length I received a muffled response in answer to my calls and I discovered two youths, neither of whom could have been above fifteen years of age, huddled in the most uncomfortable bunks one could imagine.

Their only light was an oil lantern and they were trying to keep warm with some blankets that were both dirty and damp. They informed me that the so-called Cap'n and another crewman had gone ashore for a drink, and it was clear that these lads could benefit from a good meal. More enquiries elicited that they had come from Ireland and were on their way to the North Sea when they ran into engine trouble and had to be towed in. The WRVS were wonderful and readily responded to my plea for some warm food and decent blankets.

On the following afternoon when I found that the tug was still berthed in the same place and nothing seemed to be happening with regard to repairs, I felt that something should be happening to ensure the safety of the two young boys still aboard. With this in mind I called on the Port Medical Officer, Dr. Dennis Leslie. As soon as I had outlined the position he went to work on the telephone. His enquiries led him to the conclusion that this craft should not be allowed to put to sea again until she was seaworthy and any debts incurred by the break-down cleared.

Unfortunately the Registrar had just left for a week-end holiday, but means were found to bring him back so that a writ could be issued. The next day when I called to see how the crew were faring the captain hardly received me with open arms. I was left in little doubt about the kind of interfering parson I was. With no prospect of the tug sailing for some time, arrangements were made to get the two young crew-members back to their homes in Ireland which seemed to be the real priority at that moment. When I consider the tiny role that I was privileged to play as an honorary chaplain in a very local capacity I am thankful for the world wide work of the Missions to Seamen. When, in the 18th century, the Revd. John Ashley looked out at the shipping around Flat Holme and Steep Holme, in the Bristol Channel, and sought an answer to the question, "Who ministers to these seamen?" he could hardly have imagined where his own response would lead in the years to follow. Through his own tremendous efforts, starting with a little sailing craft the *Irene* he came to see chaplains working in both the Bristol Channel and the English Channel and soon this work was to extend to Missions being established at 200 ports around the world.

Home Again

Whenever I appealed for help through the Mission's chaplain at Falmouth, the Revd. David Roberts, the response was immediate and effective, whether it was to visit a man in hospital or to visit relatives in need.

In one instance they were able within twenty-four hours to trace a youth who had run away from home and gone to sea. He had fetched up in a Scottish port where the chaplain already had a fatherly eye on him. What a relief for some anxious parents just to get that news!

'To Everything There is a Time'

My decade spent in Newlyn seems, in some respects, to have gone in a flash and one is reminded of an old Arab aphorism 'Life is but a sigh.' Yet again, on further reflection it is amazing what went on in that comparatively short space of time. Newlyn was still small enough to be personal, so that it was possible to get to know families really well. At the same time it was sufficiently large to ensure that there was something of interest going on the whole time.

Even the everyday happenings had a way of bringing a little spice into what could otherwise be just routine duties. Some of the weddings had their own special piece of entertainment to offer as well as being, quite rightly, a solemn occasion.

During one interview before a marriage, I turned to the bride to enquire as to what hymns she had in mind. Immediately I was informed that the bridegroom was going to choose the hymns. This was a bit unusual but, since I knew that Fred worked on a farm and often sang hymns while doing the milking, it was perhaps quite natural. Fred was in this case just a bit frustrated because, although he had been singing a particular hymn all day, at that moment the first line had escaped him. Then in a flash it came to his mind and he solemnly made a request for none other than, 'While shepherds watched their flocks by night.'

Since this was in the height of the summer I could not help feeling that there would be some eyebrows raised

To Everything There is a Time

among the wedding guests as they joined in the ever-popular Christmas hymn. Just before the couple were about to leave, in one of my few inspired moments I asked, "Now Fred, about this hymn for your wedding, it is 'While shepherds' you want and not 'The King of Love my Shepherd is' I suppose?" "Ah! now Vicar I believe you're right," came the welcome reply, and a slightly embarrassing situation had been averted.

Surprise could come in the most casual occasions. Going to visit a young man on the Gwavas estate who was sick, I found him in the sitting room with his younger brother David. We had been talking for only a few minutes when David made off to the kitchen, and immediately I was aware that there was something of a commotion going on in that direction. As I went to investigate I could see the doorway leading from the passage to the kitchen was all aglow and the cooker ablaze with a chip-pan that had caught fire. David had been busy running off a bucket of water. I was just in time to avert this well-intentioned but dangerous action on his part. Grabbing the handle of the pan I found it was almost red-hot. I quickly deposited it on the kitchen floor and then started piling mats on top of it. By this time the clothes, which had been airing above the cooker, were alight and the whole place was filling with smoke. The question was, should I get the two boys out of the house or continue with the efforts to quench the fire?

David was splendid. As I pulled down the clothes into a heap he applied the water from his bucket and the situation was contained without too much damage. Mum arrived on the scene soon after and explained that she had gone to the shop for some pieces of fried fish to go with the chips, but had found a queue there, which had meant some delay. We all learnt a few lessons that evening; to me it was an experience of how quickly a fire in the home can take hold and get out of hand.

My very next visit to that home was to take the elder brother, Malcolm, his Communion, since he was still confined to the house. We had just started the service and had come to the point where a response was called for

It's Only the Vicar

when a very unearthly voice seemed to come from nowhere. Certainly Malcolm had not even opened his mouth. It was not until the voice was heard the second time, and this time there was no mistaking the clear call, "Malcolm, Malcolm!" that I discerned a mina bird perched high on a cupboard in the corner of the room.

The longer I stayed in Newlyn, the more closely I was becoming identified with the various families and their lives. It was always reassuring to hear, on so many occasions, when I knocked on the door or rang the bell, a young voice call to a parent, "It's all right, it's only the Vicar." I like to think that this meant that it was 'only the Vicar,' in the sense that it was just one of the family wanting to come in, rather than that the person who had called was of no consequence and could be left to go away again.

Inevitably some families stand out in my memory, some because of the amount of sorrow and sickness they patiently endured and quite a few just because of the regularity with which they called on me. Dear old Mrs. Billet could be relied upon to be at the door each week, often laden down with things for the family bought at no little sacrifice to herself, as well as being laden down with her own problems and sorrows. No doubt it helped her to come and pour it all out each week and to share her feelings with someone and, from time to time, receive a little practical help.

Percy, from another part of the town, was another regular visitor. He would turn up each Monday morning in the hope of a little financial gain, however small and, to his credit, he was most ecumenical in his outlook since he also called on the Roman Catholic priest and the Methodist minister. Since he was so regular in his habits it surprised me to see Percy waiting for me in the study quite late on a Saturday evening. When I enquired if anything was wrong I was informed that he had come about something quite important to do with the coal which he was given each month by the Family Welfare Association. "Hasn't your coal arrived this month then Percy?" I enquired.

To Everything There is a Time

"It has," he began in his most appealing Irish accent, "and that's the point, ye see." It transpired, after various digressions, that Percy had heard that coal could now be obtained in paper bags. So, rather than have it dumped in his coal house he would now like it delivered in paper bags and put in the kitchen beside the fire-place.

"You're sure you wouldn't like me to come over and put it on the fire for you, Percy?" The same solemn expression did not even flicker and I was assured he would be quite content if he could only have those precious paper bags placed beside his grate. I did have in mind something my father often used to say about looking a gift horse in the mouth but, with my good friend unlikely to be moved by any such comments I refrained from any other remarks.

A certain marital problem within the parish went on year after year and the wife concerned was among the most regular visitors at the vicarage. Quite often this was to report the latest 'goings on' at The Pirate public house where her husband was a 'regular'. It became more and more obvious that the husband was going to go his own way, and, fortunately, the family, who were now growing up, continued to support their mother. Whenever I talked to this man about the problem, he seemed to have but one answer, and this was that he considered his wife should be in a mental institution. As things turned out, however, she stood the strain far better than he, and during the next few years I was visiting this unfortunate man in the long-stay ward of a mental hospital. His wife and family retained no bitterness or resentment and continued to visit him faithfully up to the time of his death.

One of the things about Newlyn which made it a place where you could seldom become worn out or depressed was the tremendous variety of work to be done week by week. Being able to visit the men on the lighthouses around the Cornish coast, as well as the Sevenstones Lightship, meant that a day or two could be spent in delightful company aboard the Trinity House Vessel *Stella*.

In summertime a short cruise aboard is always welcome and in the winter there were some special visits, especially at Christmas time. The ladies who formed the Ladies' Fellowship at St. Peter's helped to collect provisions to make up Christmas parcels for the men who would be spending Christmas away from home. Doreen assisted me in the wrapping and packing of these parcels for the arduous journey that lay ahead of them.

Among my few treasured possessions is a black Parker pen, a parting gift from the men aboard the Sevenstones lightship. It is so special that I have kept it just for making out the church registers and, over the years many brides and grooms have used it to witness the Holy Estate of Matrimony upon which they have just entered.

Christmas was not only a special time for visiting on the high seas, but also in Newlyn generally. Crowds of people thronged into Newlyn just before Christmas to admire the magnificent display of lights in the harbour in which seals tossed balls from one to another in the most realistic manner, camels were seen in the distance and a beautiful little galleon formed a centre-piece with its brilliant lights reflected in the still water. The climax of all this preparation and hard work was reached when the carol service took place on the fish market and about two thousand voices echoed around the harbour to the accompaniment of Camborne Town Band. Besides the widely-known traditional carols like Silent Night there were those with a definite local association, especially from among those composed by Thomas Merrit, a young man who started life as a miner and was the organist for many years at Illogan Highway Methodist Church. They would certainly include 'Hark the glad sound' and 'Lo he comes, an Infant Stranger'. There would inevitably be 'While shepherds watched' and always sung to the tune Lyngham with many rich bass voices echoing around like a roll of drums.

Little did I realize as I spent Christmas of 1968 in Newlyn that by the following Christmas I should be elsewhere, but such was to be the case. During the month of August 1969 I received a letter from the Bishop of Truro reminding me that I had been in my present living for just

To Everything There is a Time

over nine years and that perhaps it was time for me to consider another move. St. Michael, Newquay, had now become vacant through the retirement of Canon C.K. Peeke, and his Lordship thought it would be right for me to accept the living of this parish which was, in many respects so completely different from Newlyn.

This was a most difficult decision to make. My wife and I were now very much at home in this friendly parish and our daughter, Ruth, had just started her nursing career at the West Cornwall Hospital in Penzance, so that, in many respects our roots were very well established. Against this, for quite a while, I had been feeling that Newlyn needed some kind of stimulus to set it forward with renewed vigour, perhaps an evangelistic mission or stewardship campaign. I could not help feeling that this invitation to Newquay was the providential answer to my questioning, an entirely fresh field for myself and the possibility of someone with a vision of new things who would take over at Newlyn. So it was that the decision was taken to move to Newquay in mid-December.

The people of Newlyn were very kind and gave us a wonderful send-off. There was a very full gathering in the church hall when presentations were made and the churchwarden Arthur Richards, speaking on behalf of the parish, said something about our little family and the time we had spent in Newlyn. Certain families made their own individual gestures - a father and son on the door-step with dad holding a nice pot-plant. There was certainly no speech made here, but the action spoke volumes and it made me very glad to think that here was a little family united and happy - it may so well have been otherwise.

Members of the Fishermen's Rest assured me that they would be going to Newquay for my induction and, when I informed them that coaches were being organized, I was told quite firmly that they were going in a coach on their own!

The day following the institution at St. Michael's Newquay, there was a heading in the "Western Morning News" which drew attention to the large number of light blue Canon's Capes that appeared at the service, and I was greatly touched by this token of support from members of the Cathedral Chapter.

What had, however, especially caught my eye on that very special night was the number of dark blue jerseys that lined some of the pews.

Epilogue

What has been written in the foregoing chapters readers will have found to be everyday happenings and the question might therefore be asked; 'Why bother?' So it is pertinent for me to offer one or two ideas that lie behind placing these events on record.

We live in a world where many minds can be easily imprisoned and manipulated by the mass-media. People become transported into realms of fantasy which, while in one sense they know them to be make-believe, yet, at the same time they are content to be absorbed in them. Often it provides a way of escape from an existence they find uncomfortable as well as boring. Some will find that science fiction grips them and, in order that these programmes may hold their appeal, script writers must go to ever greater lengths to stimulate the imagination. Others will live in the world of the soap opera and look forward to each fresh instalment that appears on a particular channel. It seems to be the fashion here to see how many different computations of wife and husband exchanges can be arranged regardless of any thoughts of morality.

It is a great pity that the advent of television has meant that fewer people now read the world's best literature and I wonder just what percentage of our nation still cares to study the Bible. On one of my first visits to the Eddystone lighthouse I asked one of the young keepers by the name of David if he had any particular problems. He at once replied that he had and he was having some difficulty with a course

It's Only the Vicar

of Bible study notes that he was following. Just how many of the men in the country today would list this as the first problem they would like to discuss?

Against the contrast of the atmosphere of a Cornish fishing community of a quarter-of-a-century ago minds may again turn to thinking of the importance of life itself and take time for reflection on the true purpose for our existence.

It has often been said by those who visit patients who are seriously ill, they have come away feeling that they have received far greater benefit than they have been able to give. I could say something the same about my stay in Newlyn. While I may have been able to minister to them, through my particular calling as a parish priest, they have done so much for me through just being themselves.

While the fisherfolk, with whom I was in daily contact, would hardly know much about "higher criticism" and they may not even have given a thought to "realized eschatology," yet they were very near to the heart of the Gospel. Some of the men I knew not only spoke the same kind of language as Peter and Andrew, James and John but, what is more important, I believe they thought in the same terms. I do not believe either that all the first disciples were "unlearned and ignorant men," but rather that there were among them many who were well-educated for their day. The same was true of some of the fishermen I knew in Newlyn. Indeed it came as some surprise to me to discover that one skipper was a brilliant mathematician.

While I respect and value the work of many scholars today, I feel that many of their findings need to be balanced by the approach of men who have an awareness of being often in their Lord's presence, while still having their feet firmly on the ground. Through living with such men, and women, of true dedication and, perhaps above all, being in a small boat with them in rough weather, one learns not only respect but trust. In a breeches-buoy you are completely in the hands of these good men of the sea and I knew that they would never fail. Not only would I trust their keen sense of judgment and steady hands but I also

Epilogue

learned to trust their word at all times. In the same way I feel that I can trust the witness of Peter and John when they went to the tomb and found it empty on the first Easter morning.

In a previous chapter I recalled the incident when one of the crew of the *Rosebud* checked the accuracy of Big Ben by his own watch and found it to be adrift. A little incident was remembered along with the main happenings of their mission to the House of Parliament. Something of that nature is often to be found in the Gospel narratives. To give but one example among the post-resurrection appearances of our Lord: the disciples had returned to their fishing on the Lake of Galilee and that night had caught nothing. In the morning Jesus had called to them from the shore and they had not recognised him at first. When John turned to Peter and said, "It is the Lord," we are told that Peter, who had stripped for work, grabbed his coat and flung it around him before making for the shore. Peter had been caught napping and modesty demanded he should appear a little more respectable in the presence of his Lord and Master. Was he ever allowed to forget this by the rest of the apostles who had seen him struggling to get into that coat with such speed! We lose a lot in the Gospels if we fail to see a little humour in many of the situations described there and we deprive ourselves of that little bit of colour which makes all the difference to our appreciation of the incident.

It is my sincere hope that this little book may have drawn some attention to the need to look again at life itself while the mind is still active and the heart still capable of emotion and affection. When I try to consider what was so special about life in Newlyn during this particular period I become more and more convinced that it was the fulness and the richness of life within families and therefore in the community that mattered so much.

How many people do we know today who live a life that is lacking in some vital experience of what might be? Before I became a grandfather I had no idea of the wonderful new dimension this could give to life. That is

It's Only the Vicar

but a small thing however compared with the wonder and joy that an awakening to spiritual reality can bring.

Peter and Andrew, James and John could hardly have realized what a new world was opening out to them when they left their nets to follow Christ. I am for ever grateful to those who, in joy and sorrow, sickness and health have shown more plainly that the Kingdom of God is among us and that the things which are seen are temporal, but the things which are unseen are eternal.